JANET EDMONDS
BARKING MAD!

Other books by the same author

Non-Fiction

The History and Management of the Alaskan Malamute (Scan Books)
The German Spitz (published by the author)

Fiction

Piatkus Books

Turn of the Dice
Rivers of Gold
Sarah Camberwell Tring

Collins Crime Club

Dog's Body
Dead Spit
Judge and be Damned
Let Sleeping Dogs Die

Masquerade Historicals

The Polish Wolf
The Happenstance Witch
Count Sergei's Pride
Wolfgirl
Scarlet Woman
A Civil Marriage
Highwayman Bride
Flight from the Harem
The Denmead Inheritance
The Nabob's Daughter

JANET EDMONDS
BARKING MAD!

*The Adventures of a
Top Dog Breeder*

PIATKUS

None of these stories is fictitious. Anyone who thinks they recognise themselves is welcome to sue me and we'll go 50/50 on anything we can claw back from the Inland Revenue.

First published in 1992 by
Judy Piatkus (Publishers) Ltd
5 Windmill St, London W1P 1HF

The moral right of the author has been asserted

*A catalogue record for this book
is available from the British Library*

ISBN 0-7499-1184-0

*Designed by Sue Ryall
Illustrations by Julie Williams*

*Typeset in 11/13pt Compugraphic Plantin by
Action Typesetting Ltd, Gloucester
Printed and bound in Great Britain by
Biddles Ltd, Guildford and King's Lynn*

CONTENTS

INTRODUCTION

I've bred pedigree dogs for 32 years and dined out on stories about them, and some of the people they've introduced me to, ever since. I also write historical romances and publishers customarily take writers out to lunch when a book has been accepted for publication. After the second, or maybe it was the third, lunch during which Judy Piatkus, my publisher, was wiping her eyes at some of the funny-thing-happened-on-the-way-to-the-kennels stories I was telling her, she commented that if ever I wanted to put them all down on paper she'd like first refusal. Which is what she got – hence this book.

I've had a dog of some sort or another since before I was born! My mother was animal-minded. My father was not. He was, however, all in favour of a quiet life, so we had animals.

I don't know how many dogs I've had in all, but I calculate I've kept about 15 Alaskan Malamutes over the last 32 years and a dozen or so German Spitz over the last 12 or 13. (These breeds are explained on pages 2–3.) If I had to add puppies I've bred to that list, I think the figure would frighten me silly. I've occasionally looked after other people's dogs – almost always ones I've bred but sometimes others when there's been a family crisis. In addition to this I once worked for six months as a kennel-maid in a Pug and Bull Terrier kennel. I learnt quite a lot about Pugs and Bull Terriers but, more importantly, discovered that I am *not* the stuff of which domestic staff is made.

1

There have been cats in my life, too. I've had an incalculable number of moggies and for ten years I bred pedigree cats as well as dogs: Siamese, Colourpoint Persians and Devon Si-Rex. But this is a book primarily about dogs, so my cats only come into it when they impinge on the main topic – as Lucy (a very butch black and white cat) certainly did when . . . but you'll find out about *him* later.

The dogs I breed are all Spitz breeds. As many readers won't be familiar with Spitz, I'll attempt to explain their origin and the differences between the breeds.

The word 'Spitz' is, literally, a German word meaning 'pointed' or 'sharp'. It has been coined to apply to those breeds of dogs with small, erect, pointed ears, pointed faces and – usually – tails curled over their backs. Most of the Spitz breeds originate in the North, the Basenji and the Dingo being the two notable exceptions. All are closer to the original domesticated wolf than the more sophisticated and purpose-bred herding, guarding, hunting, shooting and companion breeds.

Possibly the three most unchanged of these breeds are the only breeds of sled-dog to be recognised as pure-bred, distinct breeds. These are the Alaskan Malamute, the Eskimo Dog and the Siberian Husky. No other recognised breed was originally a sled-dog even though some, like the Samoyed (originally a reindeer-herder), are now used for sledding in the occident. The Malamute is the largest and heaviest of the three breeds. It's the only one (I think the only Spitz breed) to have its ears set wide apart. It also has a very distinctive pattern of largely symmetrical markings.

At the opposite end of the size scale is the relatively small, slender, fast, racing dog – the Siberian Husky. This breed has no marking restrictions and its tail has the loosest curl of all Spitz breeds. In fact Siberian tails often hang straight down. They can also have the most attractive and distinctive pale blue eyes.

In between the Siberian Husky and the Malamute comes the Eskimo Dog, known in Europe as the Greenland Dog. It, too, has no colour or marking restrictions and is so rare in this country that it is in real danger of no longer being a recognised, listed breed. Since 1985 only four litters and a handful of imports, totalling 19 dogs in all, have been registered. It fares better in Europe but is nowhere plentiful.

None of these breeds make ideal, or should I say 'easy' pets, but all appeal to those who like a challenge and have the personality to cope.

Some of the Spitz breeds have that word incorporated into their name and two of these are the German Spitz (Klein) and its bigger cousin, the German Spitz (Mittel).

It started as quite a biggish breed, and it was miniaturised over the last 150 years until in Europe there are now five sizes. In Britain we have four but not all are called German Spitz, as they are on the continent. The smallest is known here as the Pomeranian, then come the German Spitz (Klein) and German Spitz (Mittel). After that there's a Large German Spitz which isn't allowed in this country, and finally the biggest is known here by its Dutch name of Keeshond.

German Spitz are what used to be called 'a good house-dog': they're affectionate, intelligent, make lovely companions and let you know when strangers are around.

Actually all the Spitz breeds are highly intelligent but most are also amiably bloody-minded. German Spitz (both sizes) are possibly the two most easily trained breeds, though the Norwegian Buhund must run them a close second. Intelligence and trainability are not necessarily synonymous!

Who's Who ———————————————

The publishers originally wanted me to include a family tree so that you could sort out each dog's relationship to the others. This didn't work for two reasons. One was that many of them aren't related to each other, anyway; the other was that, because no laws of consanguinity apply to dog breeding, a simple family tree is quite impossible. We decided to skin the cat a different way, with a Dramatis Personae in which some basic relationships and major characteristics are given. So here goes.

Aninrak   Malamute. Mother of Timber and Zampa, grandmother of Hank, Oske and Bayou, great-grandmother of Szminka and Gila, sister of Shan. Committed gardener and determined sex object.

Kash   Malamute. A sort of GI Joe. Father of Khan, Nari and Chimo, grandfather of Arla, great-grandfather of Safi. Piddler on judges' natty gents' suiting.

Khan   Malamute. Son of Kash, father of Arla, grandfather of Safi. Frightener of men and avid learner-driver.

Zampa   Malamute. Last daughter of Aninrak. Mother of Hank, Oske and Bayou, grandmother of Szminka. Very much a bossy-boots.

Hank   Malamute. Father of Szminka. Gave up swimming at a very early age.

Oske   Malamute. Son of Zampa and brother of Hank. A good-natured victim of circumstance and a rebuttal of the adage about old dogs.

Danny   Malamute. Canadian Champion and mother of

Zenta, Khan, Nari and Chimo. Grandmother of Arla, great-grandmother of Safi. Died tragically early.

Szminka   Malamute. Daughter of Hank and Gila. A weirdo who howled like a Dingo and had very peculiar hormones.

Schani   German Spitz. Father of Zita, Basua, Felix and quite a few others, not all of them planned. A quietly determined and highly efficient sex-fiend.

Teazle   German Spitz. Probably the ugliest GS ever bred, but loved just the same.

Zita   German Spitz. Daughter of Schani and older sister of Basua. Mother of Felix. Able to get herself pregnant by blinking.

Felix   German Spitz. Son of Zita and Schani. A dog with problems that at one stage looked like ruining his life.

Digger   Dingo. An Australian mistake.

Kaiser   Estrela Mountain Dog. A Portuguese mistake.

Tidy   Smooth Chow. A Chinese asset.

Fly   Rough Collie. A connoisseur of pasta.

Bob   Mongrel Terrier. A dog to whom Hitler's Luftwaffe was an irrelevance.

Lassie   Mongrel. The absolute rebuttal to all those petsy-wetsy theories about mongrels being healthier in mind and body than pedigree dogs, but much loved all the same.

Lucy   Fluffy, black-and-white cat. Typical inner-city delinquent and victim of a certain sexual naivety on the part of his owner.

Shiloh and Atlanta   Fluffy white cats. Almost identical brother and sister − but only to look at.

Tigger   Cat. A short-haired tabby with a well-developed sense of self-preservation.

— 1 —

SELLER
BEWARE

Being the Secretary of a canine Breed Club, as I was for
twenty-five years, is a recipe for many things, but uninterrupted
Sundays isn't one of them. I used to wonder, as the phone rang
for the fifth time between twelve-thirty and two o'clock on any
given Sunday, whether mine was the only household in Britain
that still had – or tried to have – a traditional Sunday lunch
at the traditional time.

Sometimes it would be a brief call: 'Have you got any
puppies?'

'Not at the moment . . .' and then they would ring off before
I could put them on to someone who had a litter in the pipe-line,
so to speak.

Other calls took longer. One instance is firmly planted in
my mind.

Picture the scene. The beef sat smugly on its bone, roasted
just the way I like it – crisp and salty on the outside and very
slightly pink in the middle with the juices oozing out, ready to
be poured over the Yorkshire which, on this occasion, had risen
to perfection. My Yorkshires, I have to admit, are variable. This
was undeniably one of the good ones. It was a Sunday lunch I
was going to enjoy.

Then the phone rang. I muttered a few choice phrases about
people who clearly didn't eat civilised meals at civilised times,
animadverted upon the parentage of such individuals and tossed

7

up whether to ignore it. I debated whether this call was likely to be so brief that it could safely be left unanswered in the hope that they'd assume I'd gone out and so would ring again later, or whether it might be urgent. Nowadays I'm more philosophical about the telephone, often ignoring it on the principle that if it's anything *really* important, they'll send a policeman. In those days I was less inclined to do so because, after all, one never knew.... I sighed and picked up the receiver.

'Can I help you?'

'Are you The Alaskan Malamute Club?'

'Not personally. I'm the Secretary.'

'That'll do, then. I've decided to have one.'

'I see. And your name is ...?'

'Mr Micklewaite.'

There's a certain type of man who always identifies himself – to a woman, at least – by his title. Most men give either their surname alone or their Christian name as well, but there is always that core of rather self-satisfied, lower-middle-class pomposity that needs its title. A thoroughly snobbish comment, of course, but none the less true for that.

'And what makes you think you want a Malamute, Mr Micklewaite?'

'I don't want one. I'm going to have one. It's my wife I'm ringing about.'

'Ah.' Wives are a great deal more important than husbands when it comes to buying a puppy. Husbands take the dog along to the pub and bask in its reflected glory. Wives clear up messes, wipe up puddles and sigh over chewed chair-legs; wives house-train, lead-train and car-train; wives cook unwashed tripe and lights and feed puppies four times a day; wives get their tights laddered, hairs on their good navy-blue and muddy paws on the white summer skirt. Wives matter.

'What seems to be the problem with your wife?'

'I don't know why, but she's afraid of big dogs and they are big, aren't they?'

'Yes, I think that's a fair comment. Not giant, but certainly big.'

'Well, I thought it would be a good idea if she came and saw some first.'

This was the first intelligent remark he'd made so far, and I welcomed it with some relief. Maybe he wouldn't be a dead loss after all. 'Absolutely essential, Mr Micklewaite,' I said enthusiastically. 'Tell me, have *you* seen any Malamutes?'

'Oh yes. Lots. I got this book out of the library, you see.'

Hope began to fade. 'Ah. But you've not actually seen them in the flesh?'

'No, but the book was very good. It told us all about them.'

'Then I would suggest you both need to see them before you finally make up your mind. Now as it happens, I don't have any puppies at the moment, so why don't you and your wife come over here. You'll be able to see just what you're letting yourself in for without feeling pressured into buying anything. Whereabouts do you live?'

Their home was about an hour and a half away and the drive would take them through some of the prettiest countryside in England, so I suggested a visit next weekend would be a pleasant way of passing a Sunday afternoon. Mr Micklewaite grudgingly agreed. He would really have liked to visit someone nearer – and preferably someone with puppies for sale so that he could take one back with him but when I finally convinced him that there were, in fact, no puppies in the country at that time and that he would have to go on someone's waiting-list, he gave in. After all, if part of the breed's attraction was its rarity, it was inconvenient, but hardly surprising, that one couldn't just walk into a kennels and buy one.

The pleasant Sunday afternoon's drive was somewhat spoiled by the fact that it had been raining solidly for three days and saw no good reason for giving up yet. Even so, his car, one of the larger Japanese saloons, had obviously left home sparkling with wax polish.

'Do come in,' I said, removing the dog-barricades from the gates so that they could. Fort Knox is easier to get into than any house of mine. 'I expect you'd like a cup of tea.'

At that time my house-dogs were two white German Spitz,

one of which barked incessantly, and a very large, elderly black-and-white Malamute called Oske. I had bred Oske and had him back at the age of eight when his owner could no longer keep him. He was one of the softest, most sweet-natured dogs I've ever had, cheerfully subordinate to Schani, the feisty German Spitz stud dog whose brains were firmly in his balls. But he was very large and the hall of that little house was very small. So small that one had to breathe in to get round the open front door.

I shut the yappy German Spitz, Teazle, in the kitchen but Schani and Oske were vying with each other to welcome the visitors. They loved visitors and, while Shani twisted in and out of their legs when he wasn't giving his yo-yo impression. Oske simply pressed forward like a huge cat trying to rub itself against a newcomer's legs.

The Micklewaites' reaction to this welcome was enlightening. Mr Micklewaite flattened himself against the wall and stopped breathing. His wife nonchalantly patted both dogs on the head and pushed past them into the sitting-room.

Mr Micklewaite was visibly shaken by his apparently unexpected encounter with Oske and conceded over tea and biscuits that they were a bit bigger than he had anticipated, despite the excellence of the book he had read. His wife, on the other hand, while she was unperturbed by Oske's size or, indeed, any other of his characteristics, was very definitely more than a little taken with Schani – who wasn't named after one of Vienna's great womanisers for nothing.

By this time I was quite sure they were not the right people for a Malamute even though Mr Micklewaite was still clutching at the tatters of his dream.

'I don't suppose they're all as big as this one?' he asked hopefully.

'I wouldn't say he's unusual,' I replied truthfully.

'But of course, they are very trainable, aren't they?'

'As a matter of fact, they're not. Good-natured but very independently minded.'

'But if you start training them as puppies ...' he insisted.

I don't suppose he intended the inference that I didn't and

kept back the retort that sprang to mind, pointing out instead
how very biddable German Spitz were. I didn't have puppies
in that breed, either, but it seemed to me that Mrs Micklewaite
was more than capable of managing one though neither of them
could cope with a Malamute.

But Mr Micklewaite had still not given up. It was time to
play my ace. I put my tea-cup resolutely back on the tray and
stood up. 'Well,' I said, 'you've come all this way. It would be
a pity to go without seeing the others. In any case, you must see
Kash because, if you do decide to have a puppy from me, he will
be its father. It means going up on to the garden, I'm afraid, but
I don't suppose a bit of rain will bother you – after all, when
you get your dog it'll have to go out in all weathers,' and I
smiled the hearty smile of a gym mistress assuring her pupils
that in Canada the Indians played lacrosse in the snow.

His enthusiasm visibly waned. 'I suppose we should,' he said.
'We've got raincoats in the car.'

They fetched them. In matching pillar-box red, they were
the shiny sort that funnel the rain-water down into the wearer's
boots. They look nice, though.

Now you need to know that the garden of that particular
house was very unusual. Instead of being a neat, level rectangle,
it was an extremely irregular quarter of an acre, all of it on a
steep slope – I used to call it my personal bit of Cotswold –
which began at the level of the first floor and rose to the
height of the roof. Very little of it was where it ought to
have been, behind the house, two-thirds of it being at the
side and immediately behind the cottages above me. At the
top of this slope, so that water didn't drain into it, was the
kennel in which Kash, an ebullient American dog, lived with
his more restrained companion, Szminka. If Oske was always
pleased to meet visitors, Kash was exuberantly welcoming. Just
as one needs to face into a howling gale, so one needed to face
uphill towards him if one were to stay on one's feet.

Mr Micklewaite looked doubtfully at the kennel-run and
didn't think he needed actually to *meet* the dogs inside, but
I wasn't having any of that. I didn't want to leave the slightest
chance that at a later date, when distance might have lent

enchantment to the dream again, he might make some poor Malamute's life a misery. Not all breeders are equally careful about the people to whom they sell their puppies.

I opened the run gate. Out trotted Szminka, quietly pleased to meet people but saving her enthusiasm until the introductions were over. Kash shoved past her, bounded down the lawn and with his unerring instinct for knowing which was the right target, leapt up at Mr Micklewaite in order to lick him to death before bounding off again, to approach from a new angle.

I believe I did tell you it had been raining. At the end of that first pass, his paws, which were very large, were simply wet, but by the time he had come back once or twice via a flower-bed or two, they had picked up a fair quantity of good, honest mud which had transferred itself to those lovely shiny raincoats.

'In weather like this,' I said, driving home my advantage, 'I sometimes think there's more garden indoors than out. It's amazing how much mud those paws can accumulate.'

The Micklewaites were silent. I put the dogs back in their run and suggested we return to the house. Another cup of tea seemed like a good idea. My visitors came gingerly down the steps to the drive and regarded each other's raincoats in dismay.

'I think we should put the macs back in the car,' Mrs Micklewaite suggested.

'Good idea.' Her husband had taken his off and was opening the boot of the car when a thought struck him. 'Better turn them inside out,' he said. 'We don't want to get the boot dirty.'

I decided at that moment not to plug German Spitz. The only sort of dog they wanted was one which sat in the rear window and nodded.

When they left, they were going to 'think it over'. I never heard from them again. Neither did anyone else.

Gentle Dissuasion? ————————————

It may seem odd for a breeder to discourage people from buying puppies but Malamutes are not particularly easy dogs to cope with, going through a very difficult adolescent phase somewhere between nine months and two years. With firm, consistent handling, they – and their owners – come through it with their sanity intact. It does, however, require a certain type of personality to cope. There are unfortunately far too many people who, having given in to the dear little cuddly puppy they started out with, cannot then gain respect from the muscle-flexing adolescent. There are also those who beat hell out of the puppy to teach it who's boss and then wonder why it turns on them as a young adult. In either situation, the dog is going to be got rid of and I, like one or two other breeders, always undertake to have them back. Just about the last thing I, or any other breeder, want is an ill-disciplined, possibly nasty, mouth to feed – because that's what it usually amounts to. The chances of finding such a dog a suitable home are very slim indeed and if one does come along, it may not be until years later. It makes sense, therefore, to do all that one can to put people off and to be as sure as one can be that when the puppy leaves, it goes to a home where it will stay for the rest of its life.

There are no hard and fast rules for detecting the ideal home and mistakes are bound to be made in both directions. Putting potential buyers through some sort of third-degree questioning does nothing except impress the buyer concerned that you care. This may not be a bad thing in itself but it is rarely the answers to direct questions that indicate the truth. It's the subtle little give-aways, like the woman who sits picking hairs off her skirt while she assures you that no, she doesn't go out to work and yes, they've got four acres of perfectly secure gardens. If she also fishes a hair out of her tea with an expression of distaste, she isn't going to be very happy with any dog except, perhaps, a Chinese Crested (a breed which is virtually hairless).

There are two ways of getting rid of unsuitable potential owners and by far the most satisfactory is to persuade them to go away and think it over. Nine times out of ten one never hears from them again and I don't suppose it ever occurs to them that their decision was anything other than their own. Saying, 'No, you're not suitable; you're not going to be able to cope; I'm not going to sell you a puppy,' is being unnecessarily unkind to people who, like the Micklewaites, are thoroughly decent people who just happen to have a misguided dream. Much as I dislike the idea of manipulating people in such a way that they do what I want them to do while thinking it was their own idea, this is one situation in which I feel it is the kindest thing to do.

Baldly refusing to sell a puppy is sometimes the only thing left but it carries with it the attendant risk that the person you've refused will send someone with all the right answers to get one, ostensibly for themselves, but actually on behalf of the rejected customer. This was a particular ploy of the Japanese bulk-dealers in the 70s who, when they realised that British breeders were not prepared to sell to Japan, with its appalling track record of neglect and cruelty towards pets, sent very English agents, usually calling themselves Captain This or Colonel That and who appeared to be perfectly genuinely seeking a companion dog for themselves. More often the rejected client goes to another breeder, carefully trimming his story to fit what seems to be required.

Most people do at least have the courtesy to make an appointment and I, like many other breeders, won't see people without. This isn't because I've anything to hide. I certainly don't rush around to clean up for their benefit. It ensures that I'm home and that I can arrange my work around their visit. There are occasionally potential buyers who think dog-breeders are like supermarkets – open for their convenience all the time. I well remember one particular Sunday afternoon.

The gates were firmly shut and barricaded because, among four cars parked in the drive – the most it would accommodate – there were seven or eight Estrela Mountain Dog puppies. They were the first litter born in this country and their owners had congregated at my house for a pleasant afternoon comparing the puppies and swapping experiences. The puppies were in the front garden because we are having some tea and that left them plenty of room to play with no danger of escape.

Or so we thought. The sound of someone obviously rattling the gates sent me out at the proverbial rate of knots. The gates were very difficult to open from the outside but not impossible, and in my opinion anyone stupid enough to open the gates of a garden in which there are several loose puppies isn't someone I particularly want on the premises anyway.

I reached them just as the man who had parked his very shiny Jag across the entrance managed to wrench them open. I snatched the gates from him before he had gathered his breath and fastened them.

'What on earth do you think you're doing?' I demanded. 'Did you want to turn the puppies loose all over the village?'

'Are you Mrs Edmonds?' he replied.

'Yes.'

He smiled what I think was meant to be an ingratiating smile. 'We've come to see your Malamutes.'

'Then I can save you a lot of time. As you can see, I've a houseful of guests so this isn't a convenient time. I suggest you go home and make an appointment for another day.'

'But we've come all the way from Kent!' (I was living in the Cotswolds at the time.)

'Then I'm surprised you didn't ring up beforehand and save yourself a long journey,' I told him.

'We won't keep you long,' he assured me. 'It's only a matter of seeing your dogs and deciding which one to buy.'

'Then you won't keep me any time at all,' I said. 'I've no puppies and I don't sell my adults. Goodbye.'

He protested. He was, he said, the managing director of a very large chain of garages, and gave me his card to prove it. I would not, I gathered, remain in business very long if a) I turned customers away and b) I didn't sell dogs when someone came along prepared to buy. He was quite unable to assimilate the fact that my dogs weren't a business in any sense of the word, just an expensive hobby, and that I didn't actually give a damn whether I sold a dog or not. He did eventually get the message that I wasn't letting him in because I was busy, and asked me to ring to arrange a time when he and his wife could visit. I didn't bother. I had a shrewd idea that he would break any such appointment, just to teach me a lesson and, in any case, if he was really all that keen, doubtless he'd ring me. He didn't.

There was one occasion when I had no option but to say 'No' loudly — very loudly, as it happened — and firmly. The lady who telephoned lived in central London, which is not the ideal location for any large breed simply because gardens tend to be very small. She had a Pointer and wanted a companion for it. The existence of a Pointer suggested that a garden and a very necessary willingness to do a lot of walking were present, but it raised other problems.

'You do realise that your Malamute will have to be of the opposite sex to the Pointer,' I suggested.

'No, I want the same sex. Otherwise what would I do when the bitch was in season?'

'You'd have to work that out beforehand. If you don't have a house of a design that would allow you to keep them apart without too much inconvenience, you'd have to put one of them into a boarding kennel.'

'That's all much too much bother. I'll have a dog, like my Pointer.'

I patiently explained that, while they would get on quite well together to start with, they would sooner or later fall out and have to be kept apart. Honesty compelled me to admit that there were exceptions to that rule of thumb, but they were very rare and it was safer to work on the assumption that amity would last less than a year.

'Not if they're brought up together,' she replied flatly.

I assured her that that was not the case but it was quite clear that she considered her dog-training skills to be sufficiently superior to mine — as, indeed, they may well have been — to enable her to discount that particular problem. I was not warming to her and I was beginning to have a suspicion that she knew very little about the breed upon which she had set her sights. I changed tack.

'I don't know how obedient Pointers are,' I said truthfully, 'but Malamutes aren't very and above all they mustn't be allowed to roam. How well-fenced is your garden?'

'That isn't a problem,' she said, obviously glad to be able to get something unarguably right. 'I live in a flat.'

'Ground floor?' I asked. After all, there was the Pointer.

'No, but you needn't worry: Hyde Park is only a couple of blocks away.'

'If you haven't got a garden, how are you going to house-train the puppy?'

'I shall carry it to the park.'

'By the time it's four months old, it will weigh nearly fifty pounds. You won't want to carry that two yards, far less two blocks.'

I thought that was the clincher but I underestimated her resourcefulness.

'I shall train it to use a litter-tray,' she said.

That was when I decided that the Pointer was probably a figment of her imagination. I tried to visualise the size of litter-tray a Malamute would need. An adult Malamute is roughly comparable to one of the old-fashioned Alsatians, only heavier. 'The litter-tray would take up about half your kitchen floor,' I told her, assuming that the kitchen of a non-ground-floor flat was unlikely to be huge.

She ignored that inconvenience. 'In any case,' she countered, 'even if I had a garden, I wouldn't let a dog mess in it. That's a revolting idea. The park's there for that.'

I very rarely lose my temper for the simple reason that it is usually counter-productive, but that answer – and its implications – did it. At a time when dog-owners are besieged by the neurotic anti-dog brigade who are out to make dog-owning impossible, if not downright illegal, the idea of a potential owner who would prefer the dog to foul a public park rather than its own back yard was anathema. I pointed out that it wasn't very pleasant for people, and particularly for those with small children, to have to cope with the mess left by somebody else's dog. 'Or are you going to pick it up and take it home with you?' I asked. Since this was in the days before pooper-scoopers became the norm. I wasn't surprised at the vehement revulsion of her 'No'.

'What on earth would I be expected to do with it when I got it home anyway?' she went on.

'You put it down the loo and pull the chain, just as you do with what you'd pick up in the garden.'

'That's the most revolting thing I've ever heard,' she retorted. 'You must be really sick or something.'

I don't know about sick, but I was certainly stupid to have wasted as much time on her as I already had. 'Let's put it this way,' I said. 'I wouldn't sell you a puppy – any puppy – if you were the last person on God's earth and when I've put the phone down, I'm going to ring every other Malamute breeder I know and warn them about you.'

She beat me to it: I heard the click seconds before I put my own receiver down.

One question has bothered me all these years, though. What was she going to do with the contents – the very large and smelly contents – of that huge litter-tray?

Puppy Paranoia ————————————————

At one stage in the 1970s, something in excess of 10,000 pedigree puppies a year were going to Japan, where they were being sold as a money-making proposition. Making money out of livestock is always a gamble and when these dogs failed to breed, or puppies failed to sell, or vets' bills became unacceptably high, the poor animals were turned out or just ignored. Responsible British breeders therefore became almost paranoid in their mistrust of puppy enquiries, and I make no bones about the fact that I was as paranoid as anyone.

Aninrak, my first Malamute, had her last litter around this time, just two puppies, one of which I intended to keep. I was deeply suspicious when I had an enquiry from a man with a pronounced south London accent.

'Do you have any ...' He paused, finding difficulty in saying the name – not an auspicious sign. ' ... any Alaskan Malamute puppies?'

'I have a litter,' I replied cautiously. 'Whether any of them are for sale is another matter.'

'I'll take a couple.'

'I'm afraid you won't: there are only two and I'm keeping one.'

'OK. I'll have the other one.' There was no enquiry as to its sex or the price, an extraordinary event in itself.

I was already convinced he was working for the Japanese. I had no intention of selling him anything but I wanted to know who he was, his telephone number, his address and, if possible, get some idea what he looked like. These were all essential pieces of information that needed to be circulated. 'I'm afraid it's not that simple. I insist on meeting people who buy my puppies. I need to assure myself that it's the right sort of home. When can you come over?'

There was a long pause. 'It's not actually for me,' he said at last. 'I'm asking on behalf of someone else and they won't be able to visit.'

QED, I thought triumphantly. 'And who is that?' I asked aloud.

'The Sheikh of Dubai. His daughter, actually. She's collecting dogs. She's given me this *Observer's Book of Dogs* and told me which to get. The Alaskan Malamute was one of them.'

This was a very likely story, I thought. As a matter of fact, although I had heard of Abu Dhabi, I'd never heard of Dubai and, to tell the truth, I thought he hadn't even got the name right. The need to know who he was became even greater so, working on the principle that if you want information you first give some, I said, 'The Malamute in that book is the mother of these puppies, as a matter of fact,' and before I could continue with a question, he butted in.

'Great, then we'll have her. That will really please her.'

'No, she's not for sale. She's no longer young and she's a pet. Do you have a phone number?'

He gave it to me and made no attempt to persuade me to change my mind about the actual dog in the book. I said I'd be in touch if I changed my mind about the puppy and put down the phone.

The more I thought about the phone call, the more peculiar it seemed – and the less and less like the Japanese. The Japanese are not noted for stupidity and it seemed the height of foolishness to spin such an improbable yarn if you wanted to convince a breeder you were genuine.

I consulted an atlas and discovered the existence of Dubai. I rang the Foreign Office and was put on to something called the Arab Desk. A pleasant, but slightly bored, young man confirmed that the Sheikh was in this country and had with him his teenage daughter, though he was not aware of her interest in dogs. He recognised the phone number, too. It was that of the car-hire firm the Sheikh used when he was in Britain and the owner often executed commissions for the Sheikh.

'Go ahead,' said the Arab Desk. 'You'll be able to name your own price. It's like being given a blank cheque.'

Against all the odds, the enquiry was genuine and there was no denying the fact that, blank cheque or no blank cheque, such a sale would be a distinct feather in my cap – or rather, my kennels' cap. However, other problems now came to the fore.

'I've looked Dubai up,' I told the young man. 'It's in the Persian Gulf. Would you say that was the ideal place for a sled-dog? An Arctic breed designed to live through Alaskan winters?'

There was a slight pause before the bored Arab Desk patiently explained that the Sheikh had recently used some of his vast wealth to build a new and fully air-conditioned palace, so there was nothing for me to worry about.

'That's fine,' I answered, 'but isn't he – and presumably his daughter – a Muslim?'

The Arab Desk, obviously unable to see the point, conceded that he was, indeed.

'Then presumably he regards dogs as unclean and won't allow them into it,' I suggested. 'I don't suppose he's air-conditioned the desert yet, by any chance?'

A somewhat testy voice informed me that it would be a Good Thing to sell the Sheikh a dog – both for my bank balance and for Britain.

'I'm more concerned with whether it would be a Good Thing for the dog,' I retorted, 'and it doesn't sound like it. Still, there are plenty of breeders in America. I dare say some of them will be happy to jump at his blank cheque, but I don't think I'll bother.'

The hitherto bored voice was galvanised into interest for the first time since the conversation started. 'Good God,' it said. 'We don't want *American* influence in the Middle East – we must keep them looking to Britain,' and he waxed quite lyrical in his attempts to persuade me to sell to the Sheikh.

When he paused for breath I pointed out to him that British influence in the area must be pretty shaky if it could be affected by the sale of one puppy but that I'd think about it.

I kept my word and thought about it for at least two whole minutes. Actually I thought about what I could do with the blank cheque, but saying 'no' to money you don't actually have in your hot little hand is easy enough and, needless to say, I didn't pursue the matter. It is, however, a chastening thought that my intransigence may, however unwittingly, have contributed to some of the present instability in the area.

Friends had a similar experience at this same period. They bred the very rare Sussex Spaniel, and had a very peculiar phone call.

'This is the Nepalese Ambassador,' announced a very English-public-school voice. 'I wish to buy a breeding pair of Sussex Spaniels on behalf of the King of Nepal for his private collection.'

My friend considered the possibility that the caller was working on behalf of the Japanese but decided it was far more likely to be some clever-clogs of their acquaintance who had spent rather too much time in the bar.

She laughed, 'Pull the other one,' she suggested. 'If you haven't drunk too much, you'll hear the bells ringing.'

There was a pause during which she says she could almost feel the icicles forming. 'I assure you, madam, I *am* the Nepalese Ambassador,' replied a very frosty voice.

Further enquiries proved that the King really did collect dogs in his small private zoo and a breeding-pair of Sussex Spaniels eventually joined it. You can be too paranoid.

All the World and His Wife —————————

I said earlier that wives matter. Malamutes are what is usually called a primitive breed, not very far removed from the wolf, though stories that the Eskimos outcrossed[1] them with wolves every third or fourth generation have little evidence to support them, even though the occasional crossing undoubtedly occurred. They have been pure-bred since the late 20s, early 30s which means that any direct lupine influence has been heavily diluted. Nevertheless, the legend is there. It's romantic and appealing and strikes a chord in the heart of everyone who cut their literary teeth on Jack London and Robert Service. Mostly men.

Most men grow up and their youthful dreams of mushing up the Klondike or down the Yukon are put aside in favour of the more practical and immediate ones of paying the mortgage and grappling with the rigours of the rush-hour traffic. Only when they sit by a cosy fire with a mug of cocoa in their hand and the rain beating at the window do they remember their youthful ambition, a recollection not infrequently sparked off by a television programme of intrepid young men crossing one or other Pole by dog-sled or submitting themselves to the glory of trying to win the Iditarod race. That's when they decide to buy a sled-dog, and the name of the Malamute is the most evocative.

I suspect their wives don't take it seriously at first. Why should they? After all, 'Wouldn't it be nice if . . .?' is a standard part of all of our lives. My own wouldn't-it-be-nice is to back-pack along the Pennine Way with a dog. The fact that I've never back-packed anywhere in my life and that the Pennine Way

---

[1]This is when you take a dog and mate it to something totally unrelated (usually of the same breed, though not in this case) with a view to subsequently mating the progeny back to the original bloodline (or, in human terms, 'family'). You breed the best livestock − not just dogs − by mating *within* the bloodline, or line-breeding. Mating away from the bloodline, 'outcrossing', usually produces inferior quality but can be used to correct a fault or introduce something lacking, usually in *subsequent* generations. However it is a risk because you can lose everything you've already achieved by line-breeding.

is generously sprinkled with sheep doesn't phase me one little bit. It's a dream which usually recurs when I'm reclining on a sofa-swing under the palms of a Tangerine garden and, since I'm credibly informed that the Pennine Way is not liberally scattered with five-star hotels, I'm quite happy for it to remain a dream.

Buying a dog is much easier and the vision of oneself walking out with this massive semi-wolf – instantly obedient to one's own undoubted supremacy, of course – is unmarred by thoughts of putting one's foot in the overnight mess which was immediately behind the kitchen door until one opened it and spread the mess rather more widely.

Wives are much more practical. They know who will do most of the work. They may even actively dislike dogs, though more often they have no strong views one way or the other. Many would prefer not to have one but are perfectly willing to go along with their husbands' dreams – and frequently end up more fond of the dog than its nominal owner. I remember one such situation in which the husband was initially bitterly disappointed because his long-awaited puppy (he had been on the waiting-list for two years) took immediately to his wife and daughter and would have nothing to do with him for several weeks. It came round eventually and now the whole family is devoted to it.

In short, it is crucial to find out how the wife feels about the planned acquisition. Nowadays, when the enquiry has got beyond the preliminary stage and the man has agreed that a visit is a good idea (especially since he will by that time have learned that unless I've met him, he almost certainly won't get one from me), if he doesn't say, 'And may I bring my wife?', I raise the subject:

'I assume you're married?'

'Yes.' This is usually said with some surprise that I'm interested.

'Then perhaps you'd bring her, too. I need to assure myself that she's happy about it.' They are usually quite happy to do so and invariably agree that she will end up doing most of the work. Sometimes she can't come too. She does shift work or she doesn't like long journeys. That's easy to deal with. We leave the visit until they can arrange to come together and if the reason was simply an excuse, as it often is, I don't hear from them again.

One of the more difficult ones was a social worker who visited twice. There was no denying the sincerity of his longing for a Malamute but I judged him to have far too submissive a personality to cope with one. He brought with him his own children and one or two that were in care. His own children were frightened of the dogs, though the others weren't, and on the second visit, when he had gone back to the car to fetch something, one of them let slip that his wife didn't want a big dog at all. When he left on that second visit, it transpired that his wife was with him in the car — which was parked outside a nearby pub where I couldn't see it — and wouldn't come in. 'She's very shy, you see.'

Now maybe she was. Maybe she was agoraphobic. Whatever the explanation it was clear she was less than one hundred per cent behind her husband and I was very glad indeed that I could truthfully be extremely vague about my breeding plans.

More amusing, many years previously, was the young man who arrived on my doorstep, having come some distance by train, accompanied by a rucksack and a very happy Samoyed. He was enthusiastic, he was keen, he made all the right noises except.... I couldn't pin it down but something wasn't quite right. I had the feeling that some piece of the picture was missing, though I couldn't even work out *why* I had that feeling.

At the age of twenty-eight, it is a teensy bit awkward to ask a very dashing young man point-blank whether he's married, but that was the one piece of information that hadn't been revealed one way or the other and it had to be done. I took a deep breath.

'There's one more thing,' I said. 'Are you married?'

There was a moment's revealing hesitation.

'Yes.'

'And what does your wife think about having another dog?'

He smiled engagingly. He really was a *very* attractive young man. 'Oh, I haven't told her about it yet, but she'll love it when she sees it.'

She won't, I thought. She'll hit the roof and when you've charmed her down again, she'll put up with it until it steps out of line – about six days later. Then one of two things will happen: either it will be kicked out into the garden where it will have to stay or she'll insist he gets rid of it.

'Bring your wife to see me,' I said. 'Then we'll see whether we can do business.'

I never saw him again.

A Question of Size ————————————

It's always more satisfactory if people see the breed as an adult in the flesh before they commit themselves. Books are all very well but even the best of them can only show dogs in two dimensions and all too often they are just downright inaccurate. Even when they give the correct measurements, the figures can be misleading. Heights are always given to the shoulder and it's easy enough to take a tape-measure and see just where that 25–28 inches comes on the wall or against your leg. It isn't so easy for your imagination to add the length of neck and the bulk of a head, and if it isn't easy to envisage what that height means in terms of breadth and depth, it's impossible to visualise that three-dimensional object moving around the house, pushing past you through doors or greeting you like a long-lost friend when you come home exhausted and staggering under a supermarket box of groceries.

I know what I'm talking about. It happened to me.

My first Malamute was something of an accident. I'd intended to buy a Bloodhound, only there weren't any at the time but the American couple who introduced Malamutes to this country were advertising their first litter. I wrote to find out what they were like and received back a printed leaflet with a couple of pictures. There were, incidentally, no books on the breed at all at that time, either in this country or in the States. The leaflet gave all the basic information on the breed and contained a couple of photos. I liked what I saw. The height quoted – 23 inches for bitches and 25 inches for dogs – was what the American Breed Standard calls the 'desirable freighting size'. This was exactly the size of a German Shepherd Dog, known in those days as an Alsatian. That was the size of dog I wanted. What nobody thought to mention was that the sire of the puppies, a dog called Pawnee, was from a kennels in Wisconsin where they like them big. He was a good 28 inches. Now 2 inches may not sound very much more, but when it's accompanied by a proportionate increase in all-round bulk, it is.

The puppies were getting on for six months old. Sales had been poor for two reasons: no-one in those days was particularly interested in what became known as Rare Breeds; and the Prestons were originally asking American prices – £60 a puppy instead of the top British price of about £25. Whenever I saw someone with an Alsatian puppy, I stopped them and asked how old it was, so when I decided to go ahead and have one of these newfangled dogs, I knew what to expect. Or so I thought.

That was in the days before Dr Beeching got his hands on the British railway system and strangled it to within an inch of its life. Every town and most villages had a station and it was perfectly usual to send almost all goods by rail, including dogs. Indeed, having no car, I travelled to dog-shows by rail for years.

As soon as the puppy was put on the train in Yorkshire, the breeder sent me a wire – you could actually send telegrams in those days, too – advising me of her time of arrival at my local station, about a mile from where I lived. She was due at half-past seven in the evening. By ten-past seven I was sitting on the station, waiting. The seven-thirty train came and went. No, the guard didn't have a puppy and no, he hadn't seen one at any other station. Oh, well, I thought, she could easily have missed a connection and come on the next train.

But she wasn't. Nor the next.

The station staff – there were staff on duty all night, in those days; I believe it's called customer convenience – rang up Southampton, they rang up Eastleigh, they rang up Bournemouth. None of these stations had seen or heard of a puppy, and from Yorkshire it would have to go through one of them.

By this time I was frantic, nearly in tears. I pleaded with the station staff: they must be able to do *something*; this poor little puppy wouldn't have been fed for twenty-four hours; it would be hungry, cold and miserable. The station staff were very kind. If I would leave my address, they would put it in a taxi when it arrived and send it on to me. Perhaps, they suggested, I would like to go home and take some aspirins or something. Reluctantly I went. At least I could find something to do at home.

Two hours later there was a knock at the door. I rushed to open it. No taxi-driver, no puppy. Instead, one of the porters I'd met earlier.

'That poor little puppy,' I said. 'Has it arrived?'

'Poor little puppy, my foot,' he replied scornfully. 'It took three men to lift it off the bloody train.'

It had arrived in a crate, it seemed, and the crate was far too big to fit into a taxi. The puppy was so huge that no-one had dared open the crate and in any case, no driver would have been prepared to bring it uncrated. I had better come and fetch it myself.

I went, having the foresight to take with me the collar and lead previously worn by my last, late, Rough Collie, Fly. She had been obedience-trained and a narrow quarter-inch lead had been all she needed, with a collar of comparable weight. The porter had not exaggerated. The breeder, rightly reluctant to send the puppy all the way south from Yorkshire in cramped quarters, had despatched her in an airline crate some 3½ feet long, 3 feet high and 2 feet wide. Judging by the cost of returning it, it must have weighed as much as the dog it contained.

Inside this solidly built penthouse of wood and wire was what appeared at first, to my Malamute-uneducated eye, to be an extremely large, possibly adult, black-and-white Alsatian. She appeared to fill the crate. I couldn't wonder at the porters' reluctance.

I opened the crate, called her name, and she licked my hand. She was wearing a choke-chain which was just as well, since

Fly's collar was much too small. I slipped the thin leather lead on and noticed out of the corner of my eye that the men on the station had all backed away. I'm not quite sure what they expected to happen but, whatever it was, they were disappointed.

Aninrak walked home like a lamb. A week later I realised that this was because everything was so strange that it upset her normal behaviour patterns. She had obviously never walked down a main street before and she kept close to my side as the traffic, such as it was at that time of night, went past. Once we were away from the main road, she kept halting and sniffing at everything unusual, and there was plenty.

During that first week, she had impressed me with her biddability but then her true colours began to show through and, when a cat ran across our path, Fly's thin leather lead snapped in two as if it had been a thread of cotton, and Aninrak belted after the cat. Next day I bought a more solid lead.

Although she was not yet six months old, Aninrak was as big as a full-grown Alsatian dog. She had massive, solid bone and it was quite obvious when I got her indoors that the meat and biscuit I had provided was far from adequate. It was gone in a gulp and she looked round for more. It was Saturday night, so there was no possibility of getting more until Monday. I cut Sunday's joint in half. She had one half there and then and the rest next day. We ate vegetarian that weekend.

Daylight revealed the full enormity of what I had bought. In a village full of dogs, only one was larger than she: a Saint Bernard. My landlord made the rounds every Sunday and, prior to Aninrak's arrival, I had decided that he should meet my charming puppy curled up quietly on the couch. I changed my plans. She looked smaller in the garden than indoors so he made her acquaintance outside.

Words failed him, but he was a kind man, a farmer and a dog-lover and when he did speak he refrained from saying some of the things that he might justifiably have said. Instead he commented that she was a beauty and he was sure I would soon have her as obedient as my previous dog had been.

I agreed with him. I hadn't yet become acquainted with the Malamute mind. Like many other first-time Malamute owners, I just didn't know what I had let myself in for . . .

— 2 —

ANINRAK AND OTHERS

I had always been quietly proud of the fact that my dogs were trained to a very high standard of obedience. I'm not talking about competitive obedience because I've never had any desire to exact slavishly precise submission to my will from anything, be it dog or human. I don't, for instance, like a dog which walks precisely to heel but I do expect a dog to walk on a loose lead at my side. I had always expected any dog of mine to come when it was called and to drop on command any article it might have in its mouth.

That was until I had a Malamute. I was entirely unprepared for the fact that they simply don't see things in quite that light. I've subsequently learned that this attitude is a characteristic of most of the Spitz breeds, though they differ in degree and Malamutes are by no means the worst. There's a popularly held belief that if the breed can be trained to pull a sled, it must be susceptible to training. This is entirely erroneous. A working sled-dog only needs to know four commands: those for go, stop, left and right, and it can be argued that only the lead-dog needs to know them because the others follow, although it has to be said that they will inevitably learn them if they do enough work. Even so, I've seen it calculated that any given team will only stop on command fifty per cent of the time, and I once heard a talk by a dog-handler from the British Antarctic Survey who maintained that the ideal way to go forward was

to steer the team between two groups of penguins: the dogs on one side tried to charge off after the penguins on their side of the trail while the dogs on the other side of the team tried to take off after their group. The outcome was progress erratically forward.

Unaware of Malamutes' somewhat cavalier attitude to doing as they're told, I naturally brought Aninrak up as I had done all my previous dogs and initially I saw no reason to be dissatisfied.

True, there was the time when she refused to sit on command in a shop. (This was in the days when one could take dogs into shops.) Not only did she ignore the order but when I touched her rump, expecting it to descend immediately after this tactful reminder, she arched her back instead so that it became physically impossible to push it down.

This was open rebellion and as such not to be tolerated. I repeated the order, combining it with the necessary pressure on her loins – not, as is often thought, on her spine. Again she arched her back.

By this time it was my turn to be served. I forewent it.

'Please serve the people behind me,' I told the assistant. 'This dog *will* do as she's told.'

She did, but it took time. Six customers were served before she sat, most of them highly amused. It was worth it, however, because she never tried it on again. I had stuck to my guns and made my point. From that day till the day she died, she sat on command.

It would be a mistake to imagine that there was any sort of carry-over into automatic obedience to other commands.

Aninrak had always been rather good at retrieving objects. It's a game most puppies enjoy and she was happy to fetch any object I threw and, on the command, 'Drop it,' do so at my feet. Well, more or less at my feet. Puppies cooperate with this game because they know that the retrieved object will be thrown again and, on those occasions when they pick up something they shouldn't have, like next door's cat or the Sunday joint, will be perfectly willing to give it up and, provided you make sure to play the game next time with something which is returned to them, they go on retrieving.

On the occasion in question, we were enjoying a pleasant walk along a quiet country lane, one of those narrow lanes with wide verges, ideal for riders. Aninrak was off the lead, snuffling about in the verges, investigating tantalising smells but taking care never to let us get too far ahead or fall too far behind. 'Us' constituted myself and my son in his push-chair. He was old enough to walk a bit, but not as far as the dog needed to go.

Suddenly she put up a rabbit. Immediately everything changed. She wasn't missing a chance like that. Before I had noticed the rabbit, she was off after it. It was the first time I'd ever seen a Malamute chase a rabbit. Their technique is quite different from that of Greyhounds, possibly because, like most Spitz breeds they are exceedingly bright, hounds in general being the reverse. Greyhounds hunt by sight. It's what they've been bred to do for centuries and they do it very well. This means that if the rabbit runs in a huge curve across a field, as rabbits do, a Greyhound will follow it round that curve. If it catches the rabbit, it does so simply by being faster. I've been told that if a Greyhound takes a short cut, it's considered to be cheating and in coursing this loses points.

Malamutes are pragmatic animals. If cheating gets you dinner, you cheat. Aninrak didn't waste any time following the rabbit. She assessed its trajectory and charged off along the field, skilfully timing her short and very fast run so that the rabbit ran straight into her – or would have done, had she not grabbed it and killed it before they collided. Then she trotted back across the field towards me, rabbit dangling limply from her jaws.

Great, I thought. Rabbit casserole. The dog's reward would be the bits that were not suitable for cooking. 'Good girl,' I called out. '*What* a good girl! Come on, bring it here!'

I don't know what I did wrong. Perhaps my voice was several shades too enthusiastic. Whatever it was, Aninrak stopped, deeply suspicious, uncertain whether to continue towards me.

'Come on,' I repeated. 'Bring it here.' She came a few curious steps closer. If I wasn't careful I'd lose that casserole. Perhaps I'd better make her drop it now. It was only a few yards away. 'Drop it!' I commanded authoritatively.

That did it. Doubt and hesitation vanished. She juggled the rabbit in her mouth so that it was more comfortable to hold and set off across the field, which was long and narrow. When she reached the opposite edge, she paused and looked back at me.

I called to her to come, admittedly without much hope.

She appeared to consider it briefly – very briefly – and then trotted purposefully into the narrow river that bordered the field, up the further bank, under an electric fence and there, in full sight, proceeded to eat the rabbit.

Now it's all very well to know perfectly well that a dog must be made to obey, no matter what, but there are limits, and getting a push-chair across a field, over a river and under an electric fence definitely constitutes several, especially since I had a very shrewd suspicion that as soon as I was within a few feet of her, she would charge off again.

Nor was there the slightest point in standing in the lane calling her. All that would do would be to reinforce the message that she couldn't always be compelled to come – not a lesson I wished to teach her. So I did the only other thing open to me: I continued our stroll along the lane. Aninrak knew where I was – she could still see me – and in any case, we had done this walk many times before, so she knew the way home. I wasn't really worried and, indeed, had no need to be. In a very short time she came bouncing up behind me, licking her lips. It had evidently been a very tasty rabbit.

She never, ever retrieved anything for me again. Any attempts to interest her in that particular game resulted in a bored expression as her eye followed the object, an expression that said, quite clearly, 'You threw it, duckie. You pick it up.'

Dietary Supplements ————————————

Actually, Aninrak proved rather good at supplementing her diet, like the time when my mother agreed to have both her and her daughter, Timber, in addition to us over the Christmas period. My parents' house was long and thin, and had a walk-in larder at the very end. My mother, who was brought up with animals, was a punctilious door-closer; my father, who wasn't, wasn't.

As soon as the garden gate closed behind us, I let both dogs off their leads. With the unerring instinct of those suffering from the delusion that they're half-starved, they charged straight through the house and, joy of joys, found the larder door open. They ate the turkey. That was not one of the more amicable family Christmases though I'm happy to say that my mother, who has her priorities in the right place, laid the blame squarely on my father. He did not seem unduly perturbed by this, inured, no doubt, by dozens of incidents such as one I remember from my childhood.

It was during the war and we lived in Portsmouth which, being a dockyard city and major naval port, was more heavily bombed than is generally acknowledged even today. One eventually becomes fairly blasé about bombs – after all, if they're going to hit you, there's not a lot you can do about it – but in the early months of the Blitz we were hurried into the air-raid shelter. This was initially fun, with bunk beds to clamber into, but the spiders decided it was a distinctly des.res. and moved in, dropping on to the face of whoever was allocated the top bunk. Me. We stopped using it when their presence obtruded on my mother who decided that Hitler was infinitely preferable.

However, we did use it to start with, though how secure it was I'm not quite sure because the door never did close properly. At the time we had a small mongrel terrier called Bob. He was mainly black with the usual white tip to his tightly curled tail, white paws and a white mark on his chest. His predominating colour meant that he was not easily seen in the dim light of a home-made oil lamp (the base was a golden syrup tin) that was our sole illumination.

On the night in question, the raid was a real humdinger, with plenty of noise and lots of exciting flashes outside. Occasionally the brick shelter shook a bit, which wouldn't have mattered except that it tended to dislodge the odd spider.

Suddenly, when the raid was at its height, my mother realised she couldn't see Bob. She called him. No response. 'Where's Bob?' she demanded.

We looked around. We couldn't see him either.

My mother realised the door was slightly further open than usual, wide enough for a small dog to slip through. She turned to my father. 'There you are,' she said triumphantly. 'I told you it ought to be mended. Now Bob's out there. Goodness knows what may happen to him.' She pressed a torch into my father's hand. 'You'd better go and find him. It's dark out there. He could get run over. Anything might happen to him.'

My father didn't waste his breath pointing out that, with petrol rationing, the only thing Bob could possibly be run over by was a bicycle or that a torch was useless since it was a crime to show a light, especially during a raid. He did, however, remonstrate that there *was* a raid on and it therefore was generally considered not terribly well advised to go for a walk.

'Exactly,' my mother declared. 'He might be hit by a bomb. You go and find him.'

My father went, and was gone a very long time, not returning for about an hour after the all-clear. He was accompanied by a perfectly composed Bob, neither of them showing any signs of injury.

'That took a long time,' said my mother, who had been beginning to be a bit worried, and not only about Bob. 'Had he gone far? Where did you find him?'

'In the kitchen. Someone had left the door open.'

'Then where have you been all this time?'

'I took him to see a man about a dog. Thought he'd like the company.'

Seeing a man about a dog was my father's euphemism for a visit to the local. In his own quiet way he usually turned things to his own advantage.

It isn't only rabbits and Christmas dinners that Malamutes are good at acquiring. They catch mice using a similar technique to cats – and wolves. They locate the animal with unerring accuracy and then pounce with their spine arched and their front legs ramming stiffly down to trap the prey underneath. Unlike cats, they kill it immediately.

On more than one occasion, I've had a Malamute catch a wood-pigeon but since it has always been on the verge of a cereal field not long before harvesting, I suspect that the birds had crops so laden with seed that they simply couldn't get off the ground in time.

Much more interesting was Aninrak's technique with water-fowl. At one time we lived for a brief period near the Basingstoke canal and one of the nicest walks was along the tow-path. Like most Malamutes, Aninrak loved water and she would crash in and out with as much subtlety as a lager-lout in Benidorm.

Except when she decided to hunt.

If she was in a hunting mood – and this was by no means always the case – she would trot happily along beside me until she spotted what she decided was an appropriate target. I have no idea what her criteria were, what there was about one bird rather than another that made her select that particular individual on a stretch of water with plenty to choose from. They were, however, invariably moorhens. Her ears betrayed her sharpened interest and her whole body stiffened. Then it dissolved into the supple fluidity one sees in an otter as she slid into the water and, instead of splashing noisily about as she did on other occasions, sculled smoothly across, her paws never breaking the surface, her body low in the water so that no wake trailed behind her. As she approached her selected prey, she submerged without leaving a ripple and within seconds reappeared with the moorhen in her mouth. She then, all subtlety gone, bounded on to the opposite bank and ate it. She always selected birds on the other side of the canal. Whether because closer ones would detect her ingress or whether because they were out of my reach – and this was after the episode with the rabbit – I've never known.

One of my Malamutes lost his love of water very early and in traumatic circumstances that had me terrified on his behalf.

Hank was Aninrak's grandson and when he was about five months old, I took him for a walk in a broad field bordered by the Windrush. This is a beautiful river which in many places is not particularly deep, but it is fast-flowing and with a deceptively strong under-tow which has dragged more than one swimmer under. I don't know whether the under-tow was the reason a mill was built on that stretch of river or whether the presence of the mill-race creates the under-tow, but its beauty is dangerous.

It was a breezy day in early autumn and the occasional fallen leaf fluttered across the ground until some small thermal lifted it a few yards before dropping it again so that it fluttered to earth like a small brown sparrow. The breeze didn't touch the river, though. That was as smooth and dark under its over-hanging willows as a tarmacadammed road. Which is what I believe Hank mistook it for.

He had chased one or two leaves in a half-hearted way but then one was picked up and whisked almost under his nose, a challenge he couldn't resist. He bounced at it and missed but the breeze lifted it at precisely the same moment, as if its change of direction had been the result of Hank's bounce. Clearly it wanted to play. He charged it and as he did so a quick gust carried the leaf out over the river and Hank went straight out after it.

Needless to say, he didn't catch it. Instead the 'road' beneath his feet gave way and he sank – down and down until he vanished completely in the murky waters beneath my horrified gaze.

What was I to do? He had gone down less than 4 feet from the bank and my first instinct was to jump in and try to haul him out. But I knew the river's reputation; a five-month-old Malamute puppy is no light weight dry, let alone saturated; and in any case, I can't swim. Common-sense kept me on the bank, peering into the blackness of the water.

After what seemed an eternity, the water lightened. The lighter patch became a clearly defined white shape. A shape with a black nose and two very surprised black eyes. Then his head broke the surface and he paddled desperately for the bank.

Now I could do something. I leaned over the bank shouting encouragement to him to come to me. He struggled valiantly against the under-tow and at last his paws were scrabbling at the muddy bank. Then I could lean right over, grab his neck and haul him up. He naturally didn't wait to distance himself from me before he shook the weight of water from his coat, but I was so relieved to have him back that I didn't mind being drenched. He never went into water again – and I shall never forget the expression of undiluted surprise on his face as he surfaced again.

The Cart-Horse of the Arctic ——————

Malamutes are very strong dogs. They have to be to do the job for which they were originally bred, which is hauling heavy weights long distances at steady speeds. I once coined the phrase 'the cart-horse of the Arctic' to describe them and it was sufficiently apt to be taken up by those drawing on my articles and talks for their material. Most Malamutes are not as heavy as their owners claim. Even so, a male will weigh something like 90–100 pounds and a few – usually dogs which are actually too tall to be correct – weigh a good bit more than that. If you add to those facts the additional one that, in a working situation, a Malamute is expected to haul four times his own weight – and I stress this is a normal freighting weight, not an extreme achieved only in weight-pull competition – you have a dog which is stronger than most people. It is also a breed which has been bred for centuries to pull. As a consequence, Malamutes pull with gusto at every conceivable opportunity.

When I was younger, I had no hesitation in exercising Malamutes in twos. There was always the risk that they would hare off after a rabbit or pheasant, or that a strange cat would run across the road in front of us or some silly dog want to play or, worse, challenge them to get him. None of that mattered because I always kept my wits about me and one eye on the surrounding landscape for possible hazards and if, by chance, I missed one, I knew I could hang on to them.

I lived for a few years in one of the new towns that were built in a fit of enthusiasm after the war. It was not the sort of place where it was wise to let dogs off the lead and although we were some way from a park or playing field, we did have a large patch of rough – very rough – grassland quite close on which people exercised their dogs until the builders moved in. As far as possible, I timed my walks so that we were unlikely to meet other people, and kept my eyes open for possible hazards. On the day in question, I freely admit that my attention must have wandered.

I had a lead in each hand, the loop round my wrist as an added precaution against its being suddenly jerked out of my hold. But instead of seeing the Jack Russell a few seconds before the dogs did, we saw it simultaneously – only their reactions were a lot faster than mine.

It appeared to one side of us, barked once, and charged off in the direction from which we had come.

The dogs immediately charged after it.

The sudden jerk was bad enough but I could have coped with that. The change of direction as well was what finished me off. Almost before I had collected my thoughts, I had been dragged off balance and off my feet as the two dogs galloped across the tussocky grass after the Jack Russell.

You know that scene in every cattlemen-versus-homesteader Western? The one where the cattlemen run the obstructive homesteader out of town behind a horse? Well, that was me.

I don't know how many yards we'd travelled before it crossed their minds that something was slowing them down. I suspect it wasn't until after the Jack Russell had disappeared. Certainly he was nowhere in sight when they decided to investigate the dead weight that had frustrated their charge. They stopped, looked around and came over for a sniff. Their expressions were every bit as surprised as Hank's had been when he resurfaced above the Windrush. 'Oh, it's you,' they seemed to say. 'What on earth are you doing down there?'

It wasn't until the following day that the pain in my shoulders really hit me, but the relief that my undignified progress across the field had gone unobserved was something I was grateful for from the moment I stood up. Shakily.

Who Loves a Garden ... ——————————

It is sometimes said that you can't have a nice garden and dogs. Actually, you can, but that's a whole new book. I can't pretend it's easy though, especially with a breed which enjoys the more physical aspects of gardening. Malamutes may be of American ancestry but they have a truly British devotion to our national pastime.

Aninrak arrived in winter when gardening activity was at its minimum and it wasn't until the bedding-out season that her interest manifested itself. Animal psychologists assure us that animals don't learn by imitation and, as a generalisation I'm sure that's so. But generalisations have exceptions and Aninrak was certainly one of them.

As I worked down the border, digging little holes, planting little plants and pressing the earth back round them, she would follow me down the border leaning heavily on my arm and breathing equally heavily over my shoulder, watching every move.

Right from her first day in the garden, I'd impressed upon her that the borders were taboo, anticipating the summer when they would be full of flowers, consequently she never stepped on them – at least, not when I was in sight.

Her behaviour while I was bedding-out was admirable, if a trifle restricting due to the fact that she kept my right arm pinned to my side. She watched, studied and was evidently greatly impressed by this new hobby which revealed itself.

When I had finished I went inside to wash my hands and as I glanced up through the kitchen window, I saw her going methodically down the border in the same direction in which I had worked; she was methodically digging little holes in exactly the same spots – and was methodically uprooting the little plants. The fascinating thing was that she did it without actually stepping on the border: her hind legs stayed firmly on the grass and only her front legs dug, gently.

She plainly considered it most unfair to be told off for copying me and the border was planted three times in all before she finally got the message. She so enjoyed digging that I decided that when and if she took a fancy to a spot which wasn't a flower-bed, I'd allow her to dig it as much as she liked. In the course of time she found such a spot.

It wasn't an awfully convenient one, situated as it was just behind the bend of the concrete path outside the front door.

People saying goodbye invariably stepped back to the edge of this as they took their leave and Aninrak's hole was exactly in line with the door. There were several good reasons for this, not least the fact that when the door was open in fine weather, she could shoot earth from her diggings straight on to the carpet. The more anti-social motive became apparent later.

At first it was just a hole, dug at spasmodically and filled in by me when she appeared to have lost interest, but as time went on the digging ceased being a hobby and became an obsession and the hole ceased being a mere hole and became an excavation. Aninrak was by this time slightly larger than an adult German Shepherd, and miles of exercise up and down hills had given her shoulders that Frank Bruno would have envied. The propulsion behind those digging shoulders was incredible. The excavated earth would be shifted anything from 8 to 10 feet when she was in full spate and the hole became impossible to fill in simply because the earth that had come out of it was scattered all over the garden – except, of course, for that which was indoors.

It wasn't until she actually disappeared into the hole that I realised how huge it had become. The top of the hole, the open bit that one could see, wasn't exceptionally large. The approach to it was sloping, not unlike the ramp into an underground car park, and the opposite surface edge was an overhang. The hole went into the earth for the length of the dog's body, not counting the tail. At its deepest it was 3 feet below the grass.

At that time much publicity was being given to the lack of fall-out shelters in this country and several friends suggested that Aninrak was ensuring that she, at least, would survive. My own opinion, in view of its strategic situation, was that it was designed to trap visitors who stepped back into it and so discourage them from visiting again: Aninrak strongly resented the fact that when there were visitors she was not allowed to use them as obstacles in a Grand National course that included the furniture.

Eventually Aninrak's mania wore off but we kept the hole. It had distinct uses. Admittedly we had to warn friends as they left, but confident young salesmen, who heard no bark to warn them of a dog's presence, were considerably taken aback by the sudden, silent appearance of what could easily have been taken to be a black and white wolf. They would step smartly backwards, out of attack range – and disappear from view. They seldom returned.

Flag-sellers – of which we averaged one a week in summer – were a far more stalwart bunch. Fired by the knowledge that they were being martyred in a good cause, they would pick themselves up, dust themselves down and smile all over again. One felt morally obliged to give rather more than one had intended.

Later Aninrak acquired a mad passion for carnations, which she ate, and the garden hose, under which she stood. When she was completely wet she would rush back indoors. It was against her principles to shake herself outside where there was no furniture to reap the benefit of it and besides, things that are watered grow and multiply, and there wasn't room on the sofa for her as well as us.

Aninrak had a deep concern to help maintain the health of the garden. Our landlord was a farmer who was always willing to bring a load of farm-yard manure if one requested it. This was dumped in the road outside the garden and somebody – which was a euphemism for me – had to shift it to the other side of the fence where it remained until I was ready to spread it about and dig it in. This was usually several days later because I had to wait until the memory of the sheer hard labour of throwing it over the fence had faded. During this interval, Aninrak ignored it completely. Dogs happily eat farmyard manure but I suppose she had enough on her walks, or perhaps that which is scattered in small piles along the road is more appealing than a huge heap of the stuff. Whatever the reason, it might as well not have been there for all the notice she took of it.

She became more interested when I began to carry forkfuls around and lay them on the borders preparatory to digging them in. Then she once more gave me her intense concentration. The technique was a bit different this time, though. As I spread it around the beds and forked it lightly in, she followed me, pulling lumps off the borders and running round the garden with them, depositing each lump somewhere else before returning for more. The dung was not completely rotted down and it contained enough straw to bind it together so she was able to carry quite large pieces at a time. I thought it was quite amusing and it certainly meant that she was being a real help for once: manure is heavy and if she had already scattered a fair sprinkling about, my job could only be that much easier.

It wasn't until I went indoors that I discovered that the only flowers benefitting from her care were those on the sitting-room carpet.

Only one of her descendants carried Aninrak's interest in gardening to anything like her lengths and that was her grandson, Hank. History repeated itself when, having moved to a house with a very steep garden, I decided to cover one almost inaccessible slope with the invasive ground-covering plant called variously Rose of Sharon or St John's Wort. Hank, too, waited until I had gone indoors before pulling them all out but one and when I saw what he had done, I muttered a few choice oaths and left it: I didn't much fancy going through all the contortions that had been necessary the first time to plant them in the slope without breaking my neck. This time, however, it was the plant that had the last word because within four years that one single remaining plantlet had singlehandedly colonised the whole bank and only the lawnmower prevented its invasion of the lawn above. When it come to invasive qualities, the Rose of Sharon makes a triffid look like a shy, retiring violet.

Aninrak's interest in dung went far beyond using it to manure the flowers on the sitting-room carpet. I took her for a good, long country walk one afternoon. My son was four or five at the time – far too small to keep up on foot so we took the push-chair, thereby decreasing to a certain extent my own mobility. Within half an hour we were in open country and Aninrak could safely be let off the lead.

The countryside couldn't have been quite as open as I had thought because in a surprisingly short time there was no sign of her, yet she hadn't been running off as some dogs do. She had quite simply disappeared.

I was flummoxed. I couldn't see where she could have got

to – we were walking along the headland of a ploughed field and there were no hedges. True, there were some farm buildings ahead of us. Could I have been so wrapped in thought that she had got that far without being seen? I couldn't think of any other explanation so I propelled the push-chair in that direction and I must confess to an increasing anxiety that, if that was where she'd gone, she might well find a farm-yard full of chickens.

That was where she had gone but I needn't have worried. If there had been any chickens, Aninrak hadn't found them. She'd found something else first.

She had discovered the cess-pit.

And judging by the look and the smell of her, she'd jumped straight in.

It wouldn't have been quite so bad if we could have walked home with her off the lead but since we had to go through a major part of the town, that wasn't possible, and the lead for a big, strong dog was not only thick, but relatively short. Believe me, it isn't fun walking for several miles barely 2 feet from a dripping, stinking dog. My son, in a push-chair alongside her, didn't go much on it, either.

Fortunately we had a back entrance so she didn't have to go through the house. A bath was the obvious necessity but the bathroom was, as it usually is, upstairs and anywhere indoors was the last place I wanted her.

There was only one thing to be done. I borrowed next door's garden hose and hosed her down. Aninrak thought this was great fun, especially since it turned the flower-beds into quagmires. Then I used a bottle of shampoo on her. Shampoo isn't designed to be used with cold water, but it was better than nothing.

Finally she was clean. Unfortunately she still stank. Desperate situations call for desperate measures and by this time I was, indeed, pretty desperate. I knew that once that stench got indoors, it would transfer itself to everything and would be hanging around for days.

I fetched my most precious possession, tipped it on her coat and rubbed it in. All of it.

I can't honestly say that Chanel No 5 is improved by fighting with Slurry No 1, but at least it won the battle.

— 3 —

SHOW AND
BE DAMNED

I got into the dog world by accident. I suppose you might even say by accident of birth. I had, as dog people often say, had dogs before I was born. That's to say, my parents had them, only in our case they weren't pedigree.

The canine incumbent when I was born was the terrier Bob – the one who went walkabout during the Blitz. I gather he left home when I arrived, an action which my father said indicated his innate intelligence, but after three or four days he returned, thereby lowering the level of his intellect in my father's eyes.

I've never known whether Bob was intrepid or foolhardy. He once leapt the front garden wall to get at a hot bitch. Nothing in that, you may say, but this was just before the war and the low wall was still topped with an ornamental iron chain which had spiky bits – and Bob didn't quite clear it. The vet was called and, most interestingly to my five-year-old eyes, sewed his tummy together on the kitchen table. On another occasion during the war he fell, jumped or was pushed into a bomb-crater and was only rescued when someone else's dog wouldn't settle and led her owner to the nearby crater. It was night-time, German bombers were a nightly occurrence, but the war effort was diverted to rescue Bob.

This sort of incident inculcated into me very early a well-balanced sense of priority: Dogs Come First.

The first dog of my very own cost me half a guinea and I was allowed to have her as a reward for passing the 11-plus. She was liver-and-white and I called her Lassie. (The film was just out and I was only eleven! Actually, it was a toss-up between Lassie and Flicka.) She came from a pet-dealer who had a stall at the top of Cosham High Street and, with hindsight, I imagine Whippet and Springer Spaniel played some part in her ancestry.

My father looked at her feet and predicted that she would grow much too big and wouldn't I prefer that dear little terrier in the corner? But that dear little terrier – who was probably only about five weeks old – spent all its time curled up asleep, whereas Lassie played. I stood firm. My father turned out to be wrong: she ended up about 10 inches high at the shoulder. That was her great plus. One of her minuses was that she had regular epileptic fits.

Lassie was the perfect rebuttal to all those who declare that mongrels are better than purebred dogs. When I bought her, no one had the slightest idea whether she would end up large or small, solid or slight. Apart from her epilepsy, she was the most neurotic dog I've ever owned. None of this stopped me from loving her dearly but it certainly disposes of the widespread theory that mongrels have the benefit of 'hybrid vigour' and are therefore sounder, both physically and mentally, than pedigree dogs.

My mother taught me how to deal with the fits. In those days it was simple: you placed cold compresses on the dog's head and put it in a dark, quiet place until it had recovered. It was my mother who stood up to my father's insistence that Lassie should be put down after my brother had let her out when she was in season and she had inevitably entertained the neighbours by getting herself mated in the street.

'The dogs,' my mother insisted, 'were only doing what came naturallly and you can't blame Janet for her getting out, so why punish them?'

Instead, my brother's pocket-money was stopped for two weeks and Lassie was reprieved.

Her neurosis became even more pronounced after she'd whelped. For some reason no-one made a note of the fateful day or calculated when any puppies would be due so she continued to sleep in the sitting-room where, in the fullness of sixty-three days or thereabouts she quietly delivered herself of five puppies – one in each arm-chair and three on the sofa.

By the time my mother went into the sitting-room in the morning – it was probably just as well it wasn't my father who discovered what had happened – the two puppies in the arm-chairs had become dangerously cold, so she reunited them with the others on the sofa. Dogs, of course, can't count, and Lassie seemed surprised at this sudden augmentation of her family. They had the right smell, however, so she accepted them and they throve.

What Lassie was emphatically not prepared to accept was anyone looking at them. After the first two or three peeps by one member of the family or another, she began stuffing them down the side of the sofa and sitting on them and when my mother fished them out for fear of their suffocating, she got bitten for her pains.

My mother's solution to the problem was simple and appropriately dog-minded. We would stop using the sitting-room until the puppies were up and around.

I can't truthfully say that my father was happy with this but he went along with it until Lassie decided that the whole of the very large sitting-room was her exclusive territory and she would defend it against anyone who came into it unless they happened to have a bowl of dog-food with them. The last straw was when she bit him as he was getting a book.

'That's it,' he said, storming back into the dining-room. 'I'm not being kept out of my own sitting-room by a damned dog.' This was strong language from my father, who once told my mother off for swearing in front of the children when she had used precisely that word.

I was terrified. It sounded as if this time he might really insist on having her put down.

Fortunately for everyone's peace of mind, he had a less drastic solution in mind. He appropriated the clothes-horse, placed it in front of the sofa and draped it with old sheets. He told my protesting mother that it was a small sacrifice for her to make. For the next fortnight or so we relaxed in the sitting-room, listening to the radio or reading, always with a background continuum of steady growling which Lassie seemed able to sustain for an entire evening without apparently pausing for breath.

Happily, Lassie decided that Once Was Enough and ever thereafter kept her legs very firmly crossed whenever she was in season which was probably just as well since none of those carefully guarded puppies lived much beyond a year, all being put down because they, too, had fits.

Fly in the Ointment ————————

I came into Rough Collies by almost as big an accident as I later came into Malamutes. I decided to buy myself a pedigree dog. I knew exactly what I wanted. A Borzoi. I had seen a photo of Queen Alexandra with one and I quite fancied myself as a similar picture of elegance. I saw myself tall, chic and well-groomed in a beautifully cut little black dress, a Borzoi at my side. This mental picture was unmarred by the fact that I'm only 5 feet 2 inches, look like a sack of potatoes in almost anything, have hair that (five minutes after leaving a hairdresser) looks like that of the Wild Woman of Borneo and that, in any case, LBDs don't look half so chic when plastered in dog-hairs.

I never did get a Borzoi because the breeder to whom I went also bred Rough Collies and one of her adults, a bitch she had had back, instantly decided I was hers. So she went home with me and it was through her I dipped a toe in the water of dog shows.

In those days most of my spare time was taken up with horses so showing dogs was very much a subsidiary interest and one which was initially bedevilled by the particular sod's law which decrees that if a thing can go wrong, it will.

Fly never got to her first dog show because she went lame. Naturally, I took her to the vet.

Now a good veterinary practice is worth walking barefoot over broken glass for. They do exist, but there aren't nearly as many of them as you might expect. Proximity is unlikely to be the best criterion and it's very unwise to be misled by a charming bedside manner into thinking that the veterinary expertise is necessarily of the same calibre.

My first intimation that vets in small animal practice were not without their flaws came when I took Fly and her lameness to a large city practice. Having spent so much of my time with horses I knew precisely how to tell which leg was the lame one. The young assistant vet had obviously not benefited from the same sort of background. In response to my saying that she was limping with the left fore, he had me trot her up and down, which was reasonable enough, and then informed me that the lameness was in the *right* foreleg. In order to push his diagnosis home, he picked up her right leg and pressed the fingers of one hand very hard indeed between two of the muscles of her upper arm. Fly cried out in pain, as well she might, and he turned to me, patronisingly triumphant.

'There you are, you see. That's where it hurts.'

'Of course it hurt,' I told him, 'but that's not where she's lame.'

I took her to another practice, some considerable distance away and this time all I said was that she was lame. As before, I trotted her up and down the vet's drive. He nodded.

'It's the left front foot,' he said. Close examination in his surgery resulted in the opinion that she had strained it, and that time, rest and some liniment would see it right, which proved to be the case though not soon enough for her to be shown.

In fairness to that first practice I have to say that the senior partner later diagnosed Fly's cancerous womb and operated with the expedition needed to save her life. In the course of that operation he made a comment which I have more than once used with great satisfaction on the more pompous practitioners of human medicine.

Fly was a very snappy bitch and I was dreading the day when her stitches had to be removed, the more so because I remembered how extremely painful I had found it when I had had stitches removed from my scalp after a horse trod on my head.

The vet removed Fly's stitches very quickly and without her so much as curling her lip. I expressed my surprise.

'It's perfectly possible to take them out painlessly,' he told me.

'It jolly well wasn't painless when the doctor took them out of my head,' I said.

He grinned. 'Doctors don't have to be so careful,' he said. 'After all, a doctor's patient may flinch and say ouch but he won't turn round and sink his teeth into the doctor's hand, he won't kick, and he won't try to gouge his stomach out with a horn.'

Earlier in that same course of treatment, he had made another comment which I also bear in mind in relation to its human application: on the day that Fly had her operation, I rang up to find out how it had gone.

'The operation was a success,' he told me.

'Thank God for that,' I said with heart-felt relief – it had been a very long and anxious day.

'That only means she didn't die under the anaesthetic,' he told me sternly. 'She's got a long way to go yet.'

That sort of remark helps you get things in proportion.

Fly missed her second show, too. She was getting very fat. I cut her food down as much as I dared, but it made no appreciable difference. She came riding with me and that, too, had no effect. I began running her beside my bicycle but still she gained weight. I couldn't understand it.

Then I came home one lunch-time.

I was a teacher in my first post and I lived in a large house which was entirely let out as bed-sitters. I was the only English tenant. All the others were Italian women whose husbands served on the trans-Atlantic liners and by coming to England for the nine-month season every year, they saw their husbands every two weeks instead of only through the winter months when they were back in Genoa. Those women were an education for me – and not only in Italian, a language I was forced to pick up because they spoke no English (and had no interest in learning to), and it was a matter of learn it or have no one to talk to.

They taught me to cook Italian dishes. Their method was simple: I copied them. When my turn came to cook, one of them stood over me with a wooden spoon and whenever I made a mistake – too much rosemary, not enough tomato – that soon descended with considerable force on my knuckles. I learned quickly. I'm a dab hand at pasta.

It was pasta that was the undoing of Fly's figure.

It so happened that the key for any given room in that house opened all of the others. Not an ideal situation, but we were all honest so it didn't matter in practice. I was very surprised to come home that lunch-time and find my door open. I was quite sure I'd closed and locked it before I left. I wasn't surprised when I went in to find no sign of Fly, but I was very worried.

I knocked on the door of the room next door. As it opened,

so did my mouth, all ready to ask if anyone had seen Fly. The question remained unasked because there she was, devouring with great glee a plateful of spaghetti milanese. It transpired that they'd been feeding her for weeks, ever since they discovered that she was given only one meal a day and who, they asked me, can possibly survive on just one meal a day – and especially when they were getting as much exercise as she was?

They reluctantly accepted my assurance that one meal was all a dog needed and that the exercise had been primarily intended to knock off the weight they were so diligently putting on. They promised to stop and although I was able to get her weight back to normal, I wasn't able to do so in time for that particular show.

I'm happy to report that nothing prevented her getting to her third one and she had an admiring and vociferous Italian audience. Thank goodness she took a first prize – nothing less would have convinced them that my one-meal-a-day theory was valid.

Dog Stars —————————————————————————————

When I bought Aninrak I no more intended to show her initially than I had intended to show Fly but word soon got out among the local dog fraternity that this woman had this weird and wonderful new breed. I was asked to enter her at the local Open Show – a term which means it's open to everyone, not just to members of the organising society and to all Kennel Club-registered dogs, including Champions – because they wanted something a bit different to attract publicity.

In those days very few people were interested in taking up what is now known as a Rare Breed because there was neither kudos – in the shape of the Challenge Certificates that eventually make a dog a Champion – nor money to be made from them. They still don't attract CCs but I'm afraid they have attracted the get-rich-quick brigade charging – and getting – prices into four figures for puppies bred by those with the foresight to climb on to the bandwagon early enough.

Thirty years ago it was very different. Judges weren't particularly interested even in finding out what it was and if a Rare Breed won, it did so as much because the judge wanted to create a stir as because it deserved to.

There were exceptions and as the years passed they became more numerous. The Finnish Spitz Club decided to run a show for the Nordic breeds and generously offered Malamutes − of which about three were being shown − a class, as well as the slightly less rare Eskimo Dog, known in those days as the Husky. There were less than a dozen Malamutes in the country and in order to encourage some of them to enter I myself offered three half-sovereigns, one to the winner of the Malamute class and one to the winner of each of the two Eskimo Dog classes. I can't deny that I was thrilled to bits when Aninrak won the Malamute class and I still have the half-sovereign, mounted as a brooch and with her name engraved round the edge.

Judges are human and they don't always go by the four-legged end of the lead. One very famous dog-man − and one who was actually a very good judge of a dog − had quite a reputation as a womaniser. I entered Aninrak under him at a Championship show (that is, a show at which Challenge Certificates are available in some breeds, thus enabling dogs to qualify as a Champion). He made her trot up and down in front of him not once, not twice, but three times. When we'd completed the third run, he put a fatherly arm round my shoulders.

'You're a beautiful little mover,' he said.

I looked him straight in the eye. 'I know I am,' I replied. 'But what about the dog?'

She won.

Many years later a blatant example of 'face' judging, as it's sometimes called, operated in my favour and, I have to admit, to my extreme embarrassment. By this time I was known to have some very good dogs and I'd acquired an enviable collection of Best of Breed rosettes and towels and other goodies from Pedigree Petfoods who sponsor some aspects of the bigger shows. At the time in question, I was showing a very good dog and a bitch who was pretty and sound but really not all that spectacular: there were at least five other bitches being exhibited who were better than she, including her litter sister.

The judging was illogical, most of the good males being missed, but mine won his class and Best Dog. I waited outside the ring with my bitch and was chatting with a friend from another breed.

'What's the judging like?' she said.

'Well, let's put it like this,' I answered. 'The way it's going, this one could go Best Bitch.'

She glanced down at my very run-of-the-mill bitch and laughed.

Unbelievably, that's exactly what happened, that particular bitch being placed above all of the better ones – and they weren't slightly better, they were a good bit better.

When the time came for the two to compete against each other for Best of Breed I had to ask another competitor to handle one of them. I took the dog and gave her the bitch. If the judge – with whom, incidentally, I was entirely unacquainted – was putting up faces, I'd make darn sure mine was holding the lead of the better of the two dogs. He won. When judging was over I did something I'd never done before or since: I apologised to the owners of those bitches which should have beaten mine.

Mind you, it can go the other way. Sometimes judges will put a dog down (an expression which has nothing to do with killing it, it just means putting it 'down the line' when it comes to the awards) just to prove to the world at large that they're *not* a face judge and are quite uninfluenced by the face on the end of the lead.

And sometimes you lose when you should have won. I imported a superb dog from the USA. His pet name was Kash. This had nothing to do with what he cost but was simply the word formed by the initials of his pedigree name. He became the top winning Malamute of all time in this country with a total of seventeen Best of Breeds, a position he held until he was toppled from it by his son (whom I'm happy to say I bred) who went on to gain a total of twenty-five.

Actually Kash was put down as often as he was put up, but

he was never consistently beaten by any one dog. Nevertheless, it meant that every time he went into the ring it was going to be a complete gamble. There was just one show when I knew he looked and showed better than he had ever done and certainly better than any of the competition. To my utter amazement he was beaten by a greatly inferior dog – and one which, incidentally, had done no winning before and did none afterwards. For the first time in my life I tackled the judge afterwards to find out why.

Now the breed is required by the Breed Standard (this is a written description of the perfect specimen, and there's a Standard for every breed) to have a harsh, off-standing coat. It was, and still is, a common fault in British-bred Malamutes to have a coat which is short, soft and flat. My own dogs were as bad in this respect as anyone else's and the reason I'd gone to the expense of importing Kash was because, among other virtues, he had an absolutely correct coat and I hoped to use him to breed better coats into my own stock.

The judge's explanation was quite the most illogical I'd ever heard and, in its own peculiar way, very enlightening.

'I didn't like the way the coat stood out,' he said. 'This is a beauty competition, after all, and that might be all very well but it spoils the look of the dog.'

'But the coat is supposed to stand off,' I pointed out.

He repeated that this was a beauty competition.

'So what you're actually saying,' I persisted, 'is that you've put the dog down for his most outstanding virtue and because he conforms precisely to the Breed Standard in that respect.'

He went very red and his subsequent written critique gave a quite different but equally spurious excuse – obviously he had read the Breed Standard when he got home and found out that I was correct. Needless to say, I've never exhibited any dog under that judge since.

The interesting thing is that he had on the previous occasion given Kash Best of Breed when the decision was by no means so cut and dried. His comments were illuminating for two reasons: quite clearly he hadn't bothered to read the Breed Standard before going into the ring, which is bad enough.

My guess is also that a competitor, knowing he had placed Kash well before, rang up and told him how unsightly the coat was – there are exhibitors who do that sort of thing – and he, like an idiot, hadn't checked those statements against the Breed Standard.

Some people are none too scrupulous about how they win. I remember an American exhibitor, observing that one of my dogs had what is called a 'snow nose' – that is, a paler streak down the centre of the nose leather which occurs when the body is under prolonged stress such as when a bitch is in season or the weather is particularly cold – advised me to have it tattooed black. I hadn't the slightest intention of doing any such thing for a number of reasons but all I said was, 'But that's cheating.'

'If I have to cheat to win,' she replied. 'I cheat.'

Show-offs ————————————————————

There is a firm rule that there must be no conversation in the ring between the judge and the handler. In point of fact there always is, even if it's simply a matter of the judge's asking how old the dog is. There are judges who break the rule by giving a running commentary on how often they've judged the breed and in how many countries. All one can say is 'How interesting' and wish they'd concentrate on the dog in hand. There are rather more exhibitors who do it, going to some pains to let you know that this is the dog that won this, that and the other at various shows. This gambit is never tried in the judge's own breed, of course, because every exhibitor knows that the judge knows precisely which dog it is, even though it's identified only by a number, and what it has done in the past. It occurs when the judge is going over a breed in which he is not a specialist. Only a tiny minority of exhibitors try it on, of course, and the judge just has to ignore it. After all, if the exhibitor will stoop to that level, there's no guarantee they're being truthful, anyway.

I had an interesting variation on this when I was asked to

judge Malamutes at a show near Vienna. The system on the Continent is quite different: one gives a written critique on each dog then and there – which slows things up more than somewhat – and one grades the dogs Excellent, Very Good, Good etc, but one doesn't place them in order except that if there are, say, two dogs gaining Excellent, you have to decide on first and second, then the same with those with the next grading, and so on. You're confused? Join the club!

My hosts gave me strict instructions not to let the exhibitors know I spoke German. It appeared that they were expecting trouble from one of them, a well-known stirrer, and they decided that if the lady couldn't communicate with me, she would be deprived of the chance of creating a row and be left to mutter on the sidelines which is far less effective simply because it can be written off as a simple case of sour grapes.

I had no difficulty identifying which exhibitor it was: she came into the ring as stiff-legged as any dog looking for a fight. As it turned out, her dogs were rather nice and did well so she had no grounds for complaint, though I got the impression that my hosts were rather sorry her dogs hadn't been thrown out with the rubbish – an unkind and often unjust expression commonly used to refer to the dogs which are unplaced.

Now there was a bitch exhibited there who was without doubt quite the most superb Malamute bitch I've ever seen. Belgian-bred, she belonged to an American resident in Germany. While I was finishing off my dictated critique of the previous exhibit to the young man whose job was to translate it and write it down, the owner proceeded, in a very loud voice and fluent German, to regale the steward with a list of the bitch's wins which included World Champion from a show a few weeks previously.

Now you may wonder what was the point of that since, after all, it was me who was doing the judging, not the steward. The explanation is simple, if devious, and it's a trick as old as dog shows. The rules prohibit conversation between the exhibitor and the judge but there's nothing to stop an exhibitor chatting to the steward who needs to be standing close to the judge for much of the time. The exhibitor may not be talking to the judge, but if he takes care not to lower his voice, the judge can't help hearing. . . .

When I'd finished my dictation and was ready to examine his bitch, I turned to him. 'Now that was naughty,' I said. 'You know you're not supposed to let the judge know the dog's record.'

His mouth fell open in genuine amazement. 'But we were told you didn't speak German,' he protested.

'Not as fluently as you, but I can hold my own. You should never believe everything you're told, you know.'

'But you're English!' he said. 'Everyone knows the English can't speak anything except English!'

'I'm afraid this one can,' I told him.

He was profusely – and genuinely – apologetic, and not only because he knew I had grounds to ask him to leave the ring. Maybe I should have done but I was quite sure he had genuinely believed I didn't understand him, and his bitch was just too good to let others beat her by default. She went Best of Breed and has continued to cut a swathe through the competition all over Europe.

Sometimes the conversation can be amusing. I was exhibiting a very nice young bitch under a judge who knew me well enough to know my sense of humour – and vice versa. She showed beautifully in her first class and won it. In her second class she started pacing and I couldn't break it. 'Pacing' is when a dog trots like a camel, that is, moving both left legs simultaneously and then both right ones; the correct way to trot is to move the left fore and right hind together and then the opposite diagonal. The judge came over to me.

'I'm sorry, my dear,' he said, 'but if you can't get her to move correctly, I'm going to have to reverse.' This meant to place her second to the bitch she had beaten in the previous class. It's the sort of thing exhibitors hate, and more than one has been known to kick up a scene about it.

We tried again but still she paced. He reversed the placings for this class and he was quite right to do so, as we all knew. As I was given my second-place prize-card I turned to him. 'Is this where I throw a little tantrum?' I asked innocently.

He put his arm round my shoulders. 'Let's put it this way,' he said, grinning broadly. 'You throw a tantrum and I'll send you down the ring with my boot up your backside. How does that strike you?'

I laughed. 'Sounds fair to me.'

Showing One's Nerves ————————————

Exhibiting a dog for the first few times is nerve-racking because you're convinced that everyone's eyes are on you. They're not. They're on the dog. Most people soon realise this but others never quite get used to what I suppose is a form of 'first-night nerves'. It's best to come to grips with it fairly quickly because sooner or later something will happen that will make you wish you'd never been born. Like falling flat on your face as you run round the ring.

This has only happened to me once. I like to run my dogs on a loose lead at least an arm's length away from me. I learnt this from Kash who, when he first came out of quarantine, walked so close to my side that he several times knocked me over in the road when he switched from one side to the other behind me – my foot caught against him and over I went.

At the show in question, I was handling his daughter, Nari. She was moving well and exactly the right distance from me. Then, for no discernible reason, she moved so close that she might have been glued to my skirt. Her foot got tangled up in mine and down I came, spilling the chopped liver I use for 'bait' all over that part of the grass. The only thing to do in that sort of situation is to pick yourself up, dust yourself down and carry on as if nothing had happened – only it has, and your confidence is gone.

Kash was the one who put me in the most embarrassing position of all. The judge was a very dapper dresser wearing a nice line in gent's natty suiting and something in Kash's manner told me he wasn't terribly impressed. The judge had started to examine him when the steward came over to ask something and the judge turned to deal with that. Unfortunately, he didn't turn far enough and Kash quietly lifted his leg and directed a warm, wet jet on to his trouser-leg. You won't be surprised to learn that that was one of the occasions when he didn't win.

Aninrak had a different technique; hers was embarrassing because it was what dogs were not supposed to do in the ring, but it was also, happily, rather endearing. Having the true, hail-fellow-well-met temperament of her breed, she liked to let judges know just how thrilled she was to meet them and would do her best to lick them to death as soon as they got within tongue-reach. On one occasion it began to look as if she had reformed and the judge went over her unhindered. That examination over, it was time to move up and down and then to stand so that the judge could get a final all-round look at the dog. At this stage he moved a little closer than was usual. Close enough for Aninrak's purposes, at all events. She leapt to her hind legs, rested her front paws on his shoulders and firmly licked his bald patch. What's more, she got away with it – and won.

Crufts is always the most nerve-racking of the shows. It's supposed to have the same status as any other championship dog show, and so it has so far as the actual awards are concerned. The difference is that it's the show that gets the publicity. Everyone has heard of Crufts. It has a certain glamour, a certain aura of distinction in the public mind. It's one of those events, along with Henley, Royal Ascot and the Last Night of the Proms that everyone ought to go to at least once in their life-time and most people think of it in those terms even if they don't have dogs.

'Have your dogs ever been to Crufts?' is a frequent question and the affirmative answer has the enquirer looking at the dog in question with very obviously increased respect.

Aninrak was the first dog I ever took to Crufts. In those days there were no classes for Alaskan Malamutes and just two classes for Any Variety Not Separately Classified – known to dog-people as the Odds and Sods. One class was for Novice Dog or Bitch, the other for Open Dog or Bitch. Any NSC dog was eligible for the Open class but the Novice one was limited to dogs which had not won more than a certain number of First prizes at Championship shows. Since at that time Aninrak hadn't been to any Championship shows because in those days very few of them put on NSC classes, she was eligible for both and I entered her in both.

By a happy coincidence the judge was a much respected gun-dog man, the late Mr F. Warner Hill, who happened to be the judge who had given Fly her first First Prize. To my immense delight he gave Aninrak First in the Novice class. I was over the moon. She was bound to be beaten in the Open class, but who cared?

But she wasn't – she won that as well. Over the moon wasn't far enough by half. She was Best Not Classified.

This meant that we went into the Big Ring to compete against all the Best of Breed winners in the Working breeds for the Working Group (the winner of this competes against the five other Group winners for Best In Show, or, as the press insist on calling it, the Crufts Supreme Champion). I didn't seriously think I'd get *that* far, but the Group . . . who knew? After all, I hadn't expected to walk away with red cards in both classes.

It wasn't Aninrak who threw it. It was me.

You need to understand that the NSC classes were judged fairly early in the day but the Group judging was very late – getting on for six o'clock, as I recall. That meant a wait of seven or eight hours. There was plenty to do, of course. There were all the stands to have a look at and there were all the members of the public to talk to: Crufts is the one show above all others that the public goes to in droves. There wasn't really a lot of time to think.

The crowds began to thin towards tea-time and those exhibitors who weren't in my happy position began to think about going home themselves – exhibitors weren't allowed to leave until six, the Kennel Club's reasoning being that the public paid to see the dogs and had a right to expect the dogs to be there. I was getting Aninrak ready for our big moment. I say 'our' because although it was more accurately hers, she was less aware of its importance that I was.

They called for all Working Best of Breed winers to go to the collecting ring. That meant us. In those days I hadn't learned that it didn't pay to get there too soon because the dog would get bored and there was plenty of time anyway. I went immediately. There was a very long wait during which the stewards arranged us in some sort of order. I dare say they knew what order it was but I never worked it out. All I remember is that we were standing behind a Corgi. I don't even remember which kind of Corgi.

It was the long wait that did it. The long wait and the tension from over thirty exhibitors, all willing their dogs to do well.

At last it began. One by one we filed into the big ring and circled it and believe me, that big ring was huge. The judge, the late Lord Northesk, stood in the middle on a tiny piece of red carpet and watched us go round. When we were all in the ring and had all circled we stopped and each dog went out in turn to stand on that little bit of red carpet to be examined by the judge. We were about halfway along the circle of competitors which isn't a bad place to be because just before the dog gets bored, it has its chance to do its stuff, and that encourages it to stay on its toes till the end. At this level of competition, it's showmanship that wins.

When our turn came, that little bit of red carpet suddenly assumed the dimensions of a football pitch. It seemed to stretch away to infinity. I had begun to feel ... well, a bit queasy, but the activity, the need to concentrate on what Aninrak was doing, killed that and for what seemed a very few moments I was able to forget about everything else and think only of the job in hand.

Our examination over, we returned to our place in the line. The queasiness returned. I started shivering.

'It's jolly cold in here all of a sudden,' I whispered to the Corgi woman in front of me.

She seemed surprised. 'Do you think so? I thought it was rather hot.'

My shivering became feverish, my stomach rose and fell, each rise coming a little higher than the last one. Was it something I'd eaten? What other explanation could there be?

One thing became increasingly clear. I was going to be sick. Right there in the big ring at Crufts. No, somehow that had to be prevented. I looked round the ring, hoping to see a gap in the massed faces pressed round the ropes. There wasn't so much as one single break in the crowd.

But there was a little ray of hope.

Diagonally across the ring towards the left there was a notice on the wall beyond the heads. It carried one word. 'Ladies'.

I passed a few moments fruitlessly hoping that the sight of sanctuary would be enough to steady my stomach until the end of judging – after all, Lord Northesk was well down the line by now – but it was no good.

I took a deep breath and ran, dog in hand, across to that corner. The crowds parted like the Red Sea and I was through into the lavatories and when I had stopped being sick, I crept back to Aninrak's bench, where our belongings were stowed, and wept. It wasn't food poisoning, of course, it was pure nerves. Many years later I had a visit from another Odds-and-Sods exhibitor (she had Mexican Hairless) who was by that time living in Nigeria, and she told me that she and her husband always thought of me as The Girl That Cried at Crufts.

I wrote to the Kennel Club to apologise and to ask them to convey my apologies to the judge. I had a charming, if somewhat double-edged, letter back expressing the hope that I would have the opportunity to do it again. I think they meant to compete in the big ring ...

As a matter of fact, I never have. Since Malamutes have had breed classes at Crufts, Best of Breed has to the time of writing been won either by a dog I bred or by a dog sired by one I bred, but never by one owned by me. I think it's called Divine Retribution.

Mind you, judging at Crufts wasn't much better.

Twenty-eight years later I was appointed to judge Malamutes and Eskimo Dogs at Crufts Centenary show. To judge one's own breed at Crufts is the apex of any breeder's career, and to be asked to do the Centenary show was even more special.

It's always customary to dress rather better to judge than one does to exhibit and I reckoned Crufts warranted something more than a quick root around in my wardrobe. Exhibitors might not be the centre of attention but judges certainly are because every decision you make will be mauled over on the telephone between all interested parties, except the judge, for weeks after – and every woman knows there's nothing like a new outfit to boost one's self-confidence. So I lashed out and at least I didn't have to bother about what I looked like.

This was likely to be a difficult assignment. The previous two Crufts had been won by Chimo, a dog I bred, the son of Kash – a superb dog who already had twenty-five Best of Breeds to his credit. It's always embarrassing in a numerically small breed to judge dogs you yourself have bred, especially if they're good ones because you're in what I believe the Americans call a no-win situation. If you put the dog up, you're accused (behind your back, of course) of suffering from kennel blindness – an inability to recognise quality in anyone else's stock; if you put it down, it's damned for ever on the grounds that even its breeder doesn't think it's any good. There was another dog currently being shown which I very much admired. I'd never examined him but I must confess I secretly hoped that when I did, I would find him as good as I thought he was because he was the only dog being regularly shown that could approach Chimo at his best. However, when the dog papers came out a few days before the show, his owner had advertised the fact that this dog would not be entered.

Now it so happened that there were two dogs I'd failed to take into my calculations. One is super but very rarely shown and the other was a youngster that I had only seen a couple of times, when he was very immature, because I kept away from Malamute classes for nearly a year before that particular Crufts. It also so happens that Chimo, superb as he is, does have very distinct off-days when he just doesn't make the most of himself no matter how hard his handler tries and, although I naturally wasn't to know it, this was to be one of those days.

I reached the NEC early, reported in, collected my judge's goodies which for this special occasion included a rather splendid engraved piece of Brierley Crystal. Then I 'did' the stands but it was difficult to take it all in. For the first time in twenty-eight years those show-nerves had returned. My classes weren't until after lunch so I went to the judge's restaurant early, as much to fill in time as for any other reason. Nothing on the menu much appealed. I ordered something – I honestly haven't the slightest recollection what – and toyed with it. The significance of this lies in the fact that I normally eat like a horse. I couldn't face a pudding at all. By the time I went to my ring, I was not feeling at all well.

I'm delighted to report that the similarity to twenty-eight years previously ended there, probably because the one thing you're not doing when you judge is standing around, waiting. Once I start going over the dogs, every consideration other than the quality of the dogs in front of me goes out of the window and the concentration required is such that there isn't any room to feel nervous. Instead, it becomes an enjoyable experience. At least, it does when it's a breed you know inside out and upside down. I no longer judge breeds other than my own simply because I don't think I do a very good job when I don't know the breed so well.

I had anticipated that perhaps 'politics' might – wrongly – enter into my decisions, even if only in so far as they were things to take into account. They didn't. There was absolutely no doubt at all in my mind which was the best male in the ring on the day, and I don't think anyone watching had much doubt about it, either. The same went for the best bitch, which happened to be Chimo's sister Tasha, a former Crufts Best of Breed winner herself. When the Best Dog and the Best Bitch challenged each other for the top award, the dog won it – the dog that was only occasionally shown. I was particularly pleased to see, when I watched the Group judging later in the evening, that he was still showing like the proverbial bomb and was not sent out of the ring with the first 'cut' – the name given when a judge, having gone over all the dogs, dismisses those he knows he doesn't want in order to leave a smaller, more manageable number to compare.

The aftermath of judging was another new experience. The job was done, the decisions taken, the responsibility over. I don't know what happened to the floor but it wasn't under my feet any longer. You don't need drugs to give you a high!

— 4 —

A WORD IN YOUR EAR

Once it becomes known that someone shows their dogs, that person immediately becomes, in the eyes of the rest of the community, An Expert. This is heady stuff – and dangerous. There are areas in which it's reasonably safe to generalise, but all breeds have their own characteristics, and opinions are usually better offered by specialists in the breed concerned. It is, for example, no good asking me how to stop a Finnish Spitz from barking. All I know is that it is a requirement of the breed in its native land (they bark to indicate the presence of game), but only an experienced owner would be able to advise on how – or even if – it can be trained out of them.

I am, however, willing to give fairly basic advice to novice pet owners who are puzzled by certain aspects of dog-keeping. The subject on which they usually need advice or just information almost always concerns bodily functions and the conversation usually begins like this:

'You know all about dogs, don't you?'

'Well, not quite *all*. What's the problem?'

The question always gives rise to a quick glance around the room to see if we're being overheard, while at the same time, a hand on my elbow steers me unobtrusively into a discreet corner.

The voice is lowered. 'It's like this . . .' I used to expect something quite shocking. I've learned that livestock breeders lack the gentility and refinement of the rest of society, discussing such matters openly and loudly. The Secretary of the Kennel Club, not himself a dog breeder, confided to me that the first time he sat at the ring-side at a dog show, he was somewhat shattered by the explicit conversation behind him, conducted in perfectly normal conversational tones by two middle-aged, middle-class ladies about the trials and tribulations in effecting one particular mating. As his experience widened he realised that such topics were perfectly normal.

Another Fine Mess ————————————

For twenty-six years of my life, I was a teacher and I never ceased to be amazed that so many of my colleagues who were by definition both intelligent and educated, and frequently respected experts in their own fields, seemed to lack even basic common-sense when it came to dogs.

I remember one who had become a bit of a bore about the choice of dog he and his wife were thinking of getting. They hadn't been married very long and had just bought their first house, a brand-new one on an estate with the right sort of 'image'. The husband was very keen on projecting the right image. Now they wanted to complete the picture with a dog. But not just any old dog. It, like the house and the estate, had to be 'right'. The only reason they hadn't bought one as soon as they came back from honeymoon was the difficulty in choosing between a Dalmatian and an Irish Setter. It wasn't so much a matter of which breed would suit them best – and they are very different – but which they wanted to be seen with.

My opinion was repeatedly sought and I took care to make it non-committal though I must confess to an uncharitable feeling of relief that I wasn't involved in either breed and, when several days passed without the subject's being raised, I thought perhaps they'd given up the idea. I was wrong. Along came the familiar lowered voice and the hand on the elbow.

'Janet, I wonder if I could ask you something?'

'Of course.'

'Do your dogs ...' He looked guardedly around but no one was listening. 'Do they ... I mean do they, well, make messes?'

I was taken aback. This was, after all, a man who taught biology.

'Of course they do,' I said.

'How often?'

'It depends what they're fed and how many meals they have. An adult on one meal a day usually defecates first thing in the morning and again after it's been fed.'

'And you've got three or four dogs?'

'That's right.'

There was a pause during which I imagine he was doing some simple mental arithmetic. Then he glanced over his shoulder again. We were still on our own. He lowered his voice still further, 'Where do they do it?'

'In the garden. Where else?'

His mouth indicated the unwelcome picture this conjured up. 'That means eight messes a day. I don't remember seeing any when I was at your house.'

'That's because I half-fill a bucket with water, add disinfectant, pick the messes up twice a day and tip them down the loo.'

'But surely the neighbours see you?'

'I've never thought about it. I suppose they do if they happen to be looking.'

'Doesn't that bother you?'

'Not half as much as a garden thick with excrement would.'

'No. I suppose not.'

There was another long pause which I broke. 'What brought this query on?' I asked.

'Well, my father-in-law's been staying with us and he brought his dog. It's only a mongrel. It goes into the garden and it messes. It's ruining the garden and I wasn't sure what to do about it so I thought I'd ask you. I thought you'd have the solution.'

'I have – clear up at least once a day. Twice would be better.'

'I suppose so. I don't fancy the idea.'

'It isn't one of the pleasanter aspects of dog-keeping but it just has to be done. Anyway, since it's his dog, why don't you suggest he does it?'

That, of course, might solve the problem of father-in-law's dog which was, in any case, only a visitor. It still left the inescapable fact that their own dog would produce the same situation. I didn't refer to the matter again until I moved to another job. On my last day, over the valedictory chocolate biscuits, I broached the subject.

'Did you ever get a dog?' I asked.

He shook his head. 'No, we decided against it. We're going to try for a baby instead.'

The fact that father-in-law's dog was a mongrel made no difference whatever to my colleague's dilemma but the fact that he raised the point, albeit in passing, illustrates a surprisingly deeply held belief that pedigree dogs differ in certain physiological areas from the rest of the canine world, rather as royalty are believed only to sit on white suede lavatory seats or, as was once said to me of a certain very rich and very famous dog-man, that he had been observed to eat his picnic on the grass beside his Rolls-Royce 'just like an ordinary person'. The confusion was best illustrated by a neighbour I once had.

She lived half a short street away from me and in late middle age produced a daughter who was understandably the apple of her parents' eye and suffered all the unconscious disadvantages that generally accrue to single children of elderly parents. When she was about four, they bought her a black-and-white mongrel puppy which, I would guess, had a great deal of Border Collie in its make-up. I was surprised, because the mother was one of those exceptionally house-proud women who plumps cushions as soon as a visitor stands up; the house was truly spotless and every polishable surface gleamed with the industry and beeswax that had been expended on it. It was quite simply not the environment for a dog.

'I see you've got a dog,' I said, observing daughter and puppy playing in the front garden.

She gazed at both of them fondly. 'I wasn't too keen but she had so set her heart on having a puppy that we couldn't refuse her.'

Some three weeks later, it dawned on me that although the little girl was often in the garden, I hadn't seen the puppy for some time. I naturally wondered if it had been ill: mongrel puppies are rarely raised with the care lavished on their pedigree counterparts, if only because there is no profit to made from them. They therefore frequently sicken when they change home and food.

'No puppy?' I asked. 'I hope it isn't ill.'

'No, nothing like that.' Mother glanced furtively over her shoulder and, although we weren't being overheard, moved closer to the gate and leaned confiding towards me. 'We had to get rid of it,' she said, her voice secretive. 'It wasn't very nice. It ... well, it Did Things in the house, so of course we couldn't keep it.'

'Wasn't Tracy terribly upset? She seemed very fond of it.'

'Well, she was, of course, but we told her we'd wait until Mrs Edmonds had some puppies and we'd have one of those. After all, they're pedigree so they don't do things like that.'

Teaching the Basics ————————

Another colleague had quite a different problem about which he sought my advice. An ardent Welshman, he had been determined to underline the point by choosing a Welsh breed. Since his imagination took him beyond the ubiquitous Corgi, he and his wife decided to have a Welsh Terrier and since they hadn't the slightest idea where else to obtain what was and remains a relatively unusual breed, they went to a certain very famous London store and paid approximately twice as much as a breeder would have charged them. It has to be said that it was a very nice puppy that had been well-reared and well looked after in the pet department. The problem had been there from the start but Caradoc's anxiety didn't spur him to seek my advice until the dog was about six months old.

Again the furtive glance around. Again the hand on the elbow, steering me into a discreet corner.

'Janet, can I ask you about my dog?'

'Of course.'

'It's a bit embarrassing. Can we talk in confidence?'

'Absolutely.' I wondered what on earth was coming. Caradoc was, after all, a very intelligent man, not lacking in common-sense – and the two commodities don't always go together.

'This dog we've got. You realise it *is* a dog. I mean, it's a male.'

'Yes, I realise that.'

'Well, I'm worried about him. I don't think he's entirely normal.'

Curiouser and curiouser. I'd met the dog on several occasions and he always looked perfectly normal to me. 'What makes you think that?'

He checked again that no one was listening and leaned a little closer. 'Well, you see, he doesn't cock his leg. He squats – like a bitch.'

'Caradoc, he's normal. *All* dog puppies squat. Anytime now he'll stop the squat and do it on four legs. In a couple of months he'll feel sufficiently dominant to cock his leg.'

'Are you sure?'

'Quite sure.'

'I mean, he's not ... well, he's not a *fairy*, or anything?'

'Caradoc, there's no such thing in animals. If an animal feels randy, it'll mount anything – any species, either sex, inanimate objects. Don't start anthropomorphising about it. In any case your dog is behaving perfectly normally for his age. As a matter of fact, some dominant adult bitches also cock their legs. That doesn't mean anything, either – except that they're dominant.'

He was clearly relieved but the best was yet to come. So worried had he been and so anxious to rectify his dog's shortcoming that he had been trying to train it to urinate in the manner expected of it. This was a mind-boggling confession.

'How did you set about that?' I asked, intrigued.

'It wasn't easy because, as you know, we've got neighbours on all three sides, so I had to try to pick times when they were out, or it was dark. I've been taking him down the bottom of the garden, behind the shrubs. First I tried lifting his leg for him, but that didn't work, so I thought perhaps he'd learn by copying, so I've been demonstrating. Of course, I realised he wouldn't make the connection unless I urinated as well, so you see it was really very awkward indeed.'

'I imagine it must have been. Tell me, Caradoc, do you usually cock your leg when you go?'

'No, of course I don't. In fact, it made it jolly difficult, I can tell you. I did wonder if that's why he was slow to learn?'

You will be relieved (if you'll forgive the pun) to learn that the Welsh Terrier developed normally, though I gather there were celebrations in the Evans household the day he grew up.

On the Way Out ————————————————

When it comes to asking the advice of an 'expert', even the subject of death can afford some lighter moments. I once had a phone call from a friend who had a couple of dogs, and who had had others before them.

'Janet, what are the symptoms of a dying dog?'

This threw me, the more so because the friend in question was matron of an old people's home and therefore, it seemed reasonable to assume, rather more familiar with death than I. My answer was facetious.

'They stop breathing,' I said, and added, 'Usually.'

'I know *that*,' she retorted scornfully. 'I mean, before that happens.'

'How should I know? It depends what's wrong with the dog. What does the vet say it is?'

'Oh, I haven't taken him to the vet. I thought I'd ring you first and save myself the fee. I think it's serious but I may be wrong and if I am, there's no point in paying for a veterinary opinion, is there?'

'I should have thought that was all the more reason for getting him to the vet,' I told her. 'In any case, even if I could hazard a guess, I wouldn't be able to do so over the phone.' Fortunately she lived well over a hundred miles away, so there was no danger of her bringing the dog round.

There was a long pause. 'What would you do if you thought a dog might be dying?' she asked at last.

'Get a vet.'

'Really? Even if you might be wrong?'

'Particularly if I might be wrong. After all, if I were right it might be dead before he got here.'

'Will he charge me anything if the dog dies?'

'You pay for the man's time and any drugs, regardless of the outcome.'

'Oh. Oh, well, I suppose I'd better ring him.'

I wish I could report that the dog lived. It was, however, a very old dog and lingered a few days before the vet finally gave up and put him down, but the story does illustrate one of the dangers attached to being thought to know 'all about dogs'. One is quite often asked for veterinary advice. There is, of course, only one piece of advice to offer: consult a vet. This is not because vets are infallible – far from it, but there is a good chance vets are less fallible than laymen – and, in any case, it just happens to be illegal to treat other people's animals without the necessary qualifications. Giving any advice other than 'consult the vet' would almost certainly constitute treatment.

— 5 —

A QUESTION OF SEX

There is an old saying that a dog has four thoughts, one for each paw: food, food, sex and food. I'd say that's about right, though it's the third one that gives the problems.

One of the commonest causes of concern among pet owners is that their dog – and it doesn't matter which sex – is frequently randy and mounts any object which stands still long enough to enable the dog to wrap its front legs round it. It may be another dog – it's a game most dogs are quite happy to join in – which the owners at least understand, particularly if, by chance, it happens to be of the opposite sex. What disturbs them is when the object of desire is a table-leg or the newel-post or – the ultimate horror – the leg of a visitor.

I think it was the well-known journalist Katherine Whitehorn who, when asked what one should do if one's knickers fell down in public, replied, 'Step out of them, say "You can't depend on anything these days," and put them in your pocket.'

My family's technique for dealing with the over-sexed canine who insists on performing in front of a visitor is to pick it up as soon as it starts, say, 'Oh God, he's at it again,' and shut the dog in the kitchen where it can do whatever it likes with impunity.

My mother once had a Yorkshire Terrier bitch that insisted on 'mating' one of those draught-excluders shaped like an elongated Dachshund. She said it only ever did it when the more self-consciously refined old ladies of her acquaintance came to tea. She also took the entirely reasonable view that if they didn't like it, they needn't come again.

A friend in partnership with whom I breed German Spitz has a similar problem, also with a bitch, but Minty isn't interested in draught-excluders. Goodness me, no. For her it's the cat or nothing. The cat sighs like a Victorian wife thinking of England and then, when she figures it's gone on long enough, jumps out of reach. Julie says it isn't the little old ladies who are put out by such behaviour, it's men.

Dogs, by which I mean males, can be far worse. I know two very genteel elderly sisters whose Pekinese clamped his front feet firmly round the leg of any male visitor and 'mated' away. Unclamping him was rather like trying to unpeel Velcro, and ladylike admonitions of 'Naughty boy' had little effect – a fact which surprised no one but his owners. They gave up in the end and returned him to his breeder on the grounds that he was 'unsatisfactory'. Since he was rather a nice little dog, she was happy to use him at stud and confided to me that she found him entirely satisfactory.

'At least he doesn't have to be told what it's for,' she said.

Although it's a game both sexes play, there's no denying it's commoner among males and the usual advice for curing it is castration. Now I've never had a dog castrated for that reason, so I don't know whether it works, but I have my reservations. In my experience, castrated dogs are perfectly happy to mate in-season bitches, so the operation certainly doesn't destroy the libido entirely; in fact, such dogs are extremely useful because the in-season bitch is kept happy (and quiet) without the attendant risk of unwanted puppies. Anyone who has a dog castrated to cure behavioural problems should always remember two things. The first is that there is no guarantee it will work. The second is that, if it does, any improvement will come very gradually and will certainly be a matter of months rather than days. You can't hurry hormones.

It's a Tie ————————————————————————

If my former teaching colleagues are anything to go by, twenty-five per cent of the population of these islands must be completely mystified by one aspect or another of the world of dogs. One such had bought herself a very nice young Weimaraner which she intended to show and accordingly she very wisely took it to ringcraft classes where, being a sensible woman, she listened in order to learn. A conversation on mating left her puzzled. She waited until a break when there were no men in the room and came over to sit beside me.

She only glanced briefly around, but she lowered her voice in the standard way when asking The Expert. 'Can I ask you something?'

'Of course.'

'At training class they've been talking a lot about mating dogs but they keep going on about a tie and whether they were easy to turn and I haven't a clue what they mean. I can't ask because I'd feel such a fool not knowing.'

Now the simple answer to this question is to invite the enquirer to witness a mating. Unfortunately, that is unlikely to be possible and it's hellish difficult to explain in words. The tie is simple enough: dogs' genitalia are not the same as that of humans and once the male has penetrated the female, his penis – which has a small bone inside it – swells up inside the bitch and they can't be separated until the swelling subsides. This is the 'tie'. It can last anything from a few minutes to a good half-hour and breeders regard it as very important because, although conception can occur without it – an unusual but not a rare occurrence – a good, long tie is a better guarantee of a nice, big litter. It is, incidentally, the reason why throwing buckets of water over mating strays will have no effect whatsoever, and why trying to pull them apart could do permanent damage to both partners.

Since it would be exhausting for the male to attempt to stay on his hind legs, gripping the female round her loins with his forepaws, dogs have developed the technique of turning themselves round so that they are back to back with all four feet on the ground while remaining tied. The manoeuvre by which this is achieved is difficult to explain but relatively easy to demonstrate – so I did, using a handy coffee-table as the bitch. In order to turn, one front leg and then one hind leg have to be lifted over the bitch's back. I don't know how long it took dogs to evolve the technique but, believe me, it isn't easy.

By the time we reached the actual demonstration, the rest of those present had become an intrigued audience. This meant that waves of laughter rolled down the short corridor and it wasn't very long before the male portion of the staff drifted in to discover the source of the hilarity. By the time they arrived, however, we were all sitting back in our chairs, wiping away the tears and the men never did discover what it was all about.

The Silly Season ────────────────────

The whole business of seasons is fraught with complications, many of them unforeseen. Every book you read, every vet to whom you speak, and almost every dog-breeder will tell you that bitches come into season at six-monthly intervals and it lasts for three weeks. This is roughly correct. Indeed, I believe there are bitches who follow the rule so precisely that you can set your calendar by them. I can only say that I've never owned one. Malamutes can vary from four-monthly intervals (which is a confounded nuisance) to the once-a-year of primitive dogs. The most extreme case I ever owned did not come into season at all until she was three years old (between seven and nine months is more usual), her season lasted just one week and recurred at yearly intervals. It was the vet's opinion that she was almost certainly infertile. We could have treated this with hormones, of course, much as they do with women, but that would have meant the characteristic being passed on to at least some of her offspring so, since I can see no justification whatever for perpetuating what would otherwise be a self-limiting abnormality, I decided to leave it be. She lived with a young American dog whom she bossed unmercifully and I never bothered to move her when she was in season. Although he mated her perfunctorily at each season, there were no puppies until suddenly, when she was relatively elderly, she proved in whelp. Naturally, she had all the nourishment and vitamin supplements she needed but nature in her infinite wisdom had the last word. The entire litter was born a fortnight prematurely and they were all either dead at birth or died almost immediately. I should perhaps add that puppies more than a week premature are not usually viable anyway.

Many German Spitz bitches have quite a different problem. They have what are called 'silent' seasons. They come into season, all right, but there is no blood or 'colour' to tell you so and since their profuse petticoats hide the other outward sign, the swelling of the vulva, the owner can be entirely unaware. This is annoying enough if you are hoping to have the bitch mated, since it is crucial to try to 'catch' her on her day(s) of maximum fertility. It is possibly even more so if all your dogs of both sexes live together in the house, as mine do. German Spitz males do not lack libido and with one of my bitches, the first sign I had that she was in season was when she said 'Ouch' and she and my stud-dog were tied.

There are two things you can do about this when you've stopped cursing your own stupidity. You can let the pregnancy take its course or the bitch can be given an injection (known as a misalliance injection) to stop it. Both options bring their own problems. Although bitches come into season twice a year, it is not generally regarded as in a bitch's best interest to allow her to have a litter every six months. Once a year is better and, if litters are small, two seasons out of three is usually regarded as acceptable. On the other hand, the misalliance injection is, bluntly, messing about with hormones and the long-term effects of messing with hormones more than very occasionally can be disastrous, as I discovered when, on veterinary advice, I put a Malamute bitch, Zampa, on a standard season-suppressant at every season for years rather than spay her. Another side-effect is that the misalliance injection actually extends the season by up to a week. This is all very well if you happen to know when the season started and therefore when it was due to end anyway, but with silent seasons that is precisely what you *don't* know and believe me, it makes life very difficult.

So, for about three years, Zita was mated at each season. Sometimes I let the pregnancy go ahead and sometimes I stopped it but I'm happy to be able to report that eventually I was able to spot those initial indications of interest from the stud-dog and step in in time. This may make me seem a complete twit and, worse, an unobservant twit, but the dog concerned, Schani, is not only very quick off the mark, but he also exhibits almost no untoward interest until he judges the bitch to be ready for mating – and contrary to popular belief, bitches aren't ready for the whole of the three week season.

If it is unwise to generalise about the purely physical aspects of bitches' seasons, it is downright misleading to do so about their behaviour. At one extreme there can be those like my grandmother's Yeo who would tear down the curtains in her efforts – usually successful – to get out, and those like R. F. Delderfield's Punch of whom he wrote, 'If a dog approaches her hopefully, she snarls, and if a bitch yaps at her she goes her way with the holier-than-thou expression of an elderly spinster in charge of a home for fallen women.' I have had bitches who waved their back end enticingly towards any dog they see, in a manner reminiscent of Marilyn Monroe's pelvic wriggle, and others who could take it or leave it.

Aninrak, my first Malamute, fell somewhere between the two extremes. Her first season came very early for a large breed – at six months – and the village dogs displayed no interest whatever, a fact which I realise with hindsight lulled me into a very false sense of security because things were rather different next time. My fences were only 2 feet 6 inches high and if that strikes you as ridiculously low, I have to say that Malamutes do not jump. As a rule. Of course, village dogs jumped *in* from time to time but I chased them out and she never made the smallest attempt to follow them. When she was in season, however, I made sure she was never in the garden unsupervised. Unfortunately, my idea of supervision proved to be just a teensy bit inadequate.

One morning, about half way through her season I let her out into the garden. It was a bit too chilly to want to stand around while she investigated every overnight smell prior to doing what she had been sent out for, so I went back indoors, made a cup of tea and sat in the window-seat to drink it, labouring under the fond delusion that I was keeping an eye on her.

With the best will in the world, one's attention is prone to wander and mine did, though I haven't the slightest recollection where it went. All I remember is glancing up just in time to catch sight of the whisk of her tail as she cleared the fence in the wake of a leggy black-and-white philanderer of unspecified genealogy.

A Minute Man couldn't have left home faster than me. I raced after them down the narrow lane, turned left at the end and ran over the narrow bridge and then along the main Portsmouth-Southampton road, crowded at this time with traffic carrying people to work.

Still those dogs ran on unconcerned while I struggled to keep them in sight, my throat aching and my heart pumping so hard against my ribs that it was difficult to decide which hurt most.

The dogs crossed the main road and charged up an alley between the houses of a new estate. I followed. The alley ran uphill and by the time I reached the top, I was exhausted and just about ready to give up. It appeared that the dogs had given up, too. They had stopped running and were circling each other, the male stiff-legged, keen, Aninrak coy.

I knew that even if I had had any breath left, Aninrak would have ignored any attempt to call her to me. I also knew that any sudden move would send the other dog off with Aninrak after him and, while I might be ready to drop, I couldn't delude myself that they didn't have several more miles in them if the need arose. No, subtlety and stealth were called for. I sneaked up quietly and as unostentatiously as possible and grabbed her collar. Holding it firmly (and blessing the fact that she was wearing one) I snatched up a stick from the hedgerow and lashed out at the would-be paramour, catching him a hard blow on the rump. I hoped his owner lived nearby and had seen it. I was far too winded to start back straightaway, so I sat down on grass by the alley for a few minutes until I could breathe fairly comfortably again. I kept a firm grip on the collar. Eventually I felt able to move so we started off homewards.

Aninrak was tall enough for her collar to be on the same level as my hand, so there was no need for the discomfort of bending down and, in fact, I could walk home looking quite natural, as if I was taking the dog for a walk in the normal, time-honoured way. It wasn't until we reached the main road again, where the work-bound cars were still streaming past that I noticed their drivers were staring at me with a curious half-grin and I realised what sort of picture I presented. I was strolling nonchalantly along the road with a very large dog – and wearing a full-length black nylon nightie (the sort with slits up either side) over which I had – thank God – put on a three-quarter-length housecoat when I got out of bed.

I don't know what the work-force said when it reached its various destinations and, if it was anything like the comments in the village over the ensuing few weeks, that's probably just as well.

It pays never to take anything for granted when that third thought enters the canine mind. In the early years of Malamutes we had a breeder, a dyed-in-the-wool dog-woman whose rather splendid kennels were beautifully set out and maintained at the end of the large garden in a position where she could keep an eye on them from the kitchen window of her bungalow, a window at which – fortunately, as it transpired – she spent a great deal of her time. She had several other breeds, among which were Dachshunds and when Aninrak's sister Shan came into season, she moved her from the dog with whom she normally lived and put her with her Dachshund stud-dog. It seemed reasonable to assume that, no matter how willing both the spirit and the flesh might be, the logistics would defeat any attempt at misalliance.

Imagine her horror at glancing up from the dishes to see Shan sitting down but very actively wriggling her enticing rear towards the dog in such a way that copulation was very definitely a possibility even if the position owed more to the *Kuma Sutra* than *The Mating and Whelping of Dogs*. She told me later that she had never, ever, left her kitchen faster than she did on that occasion.

— 6 —

VETTING
THE BOOKS

There's a generally held view that breeding dogs is a passport to making money. I suppose, if you breed for the laboratories or have the gall to ask well into four figures for your puppies, that may be so, but only a handful of breeders come into those categories.

The way the public looks at it, it's simple: mate the bitch, have puppies, buy a few extra tins of dog-food for a week or two, sell the puppies and, hey presto, holidays in Barbados.

It doesn't work like that. I keep books for my dog-activities and I can truthfully say that in over thirty years there has only been one in which I broke even and none in which I made a profit. When I gave up teaching to become a full-time writer (and thereby self-employed with the benefit of Schedule D taxation), I asked my accountant if I could off-set my dog losses against my writing income. I dug out twenty years of account books and gave them to him. When he'd had time to read them, he rang me.

'Do you realise that if you didn't have dogs but had invested that money instead, you'd be a very rich woman indeed?' he asked.

He also told me I hadn't a hope in hell of off-setting those expenses because he couldn't even begin to make a case that would suggest I went about it in anything remotely resembling a businesslike manner.

'But you must let me know if ever you do make a profit,' he went on. 'That will be liable to tax.'

I figure it differently. If I've *lost* money for thirty years, then I'm morally entitled to make a tax-free profit for another thirty. After that, I'll cheerfully declare it. I'm told the Inland Revenue won't see it that way. I can't say I'm unduly worried. Let me put it this way: I'm not borrowing so much as the price of one paper-clip against the expectation of my dogs making a profit.

So where does the money go? The bitch (who has to be bought in the first place) has to be fed all the year round, not just when she's got puppies. There's a stud fee to be paid or, if you own the dog, he also has to be fed, to say nothing of having been bought (or bred) in the first place. There are petrol bills, dog shows, advertising, and Kennel Club fees. There's bedding and food-bowls and quite possibly, kennelling, too. Nor is there any money to be made by winning at dog shows – with one or two notable exceptions, no prize-money is paid these days and entry fees at Championship level are rarely less than £10 a dog.

Then there's the fact that things can go wrong, leaving you even further out of pocket.

Aninrak's first litter produced five puppies, three of which were what we call 'mis-marks'. This is a term given to dogs whose pattern of markings doesn't conform to what is laid down in the Breed Standard (the written description of the ideal dog of that breed): such puppies should only be sold at very low prices, without papers. The sire of that litter died in a traffic accident soon afterwards which left only one adult male Malamute in the country – Aninrak's brother. The owner assured me that he knew all about mating dogs because he'd been in the Air Force. (The significance of this qualification escaped me at the time and escapes me still.) So I travelled by train from Stevenage to Bangor – no easy journey even in pre-Beeching days – to get her mated.

It soon transpired that the stud-dog owner's idea of mating dogs was to borrow a loose-box from a nearby stable, stick both animals in it and go off to the pub, leaving them to get on with it.

What neither of us knew was that Malamutes can be very choosy. Some males will only mate the bitch they live with.

Some will mate any bitch *except* the one they live with. Others are just choosy. And the same goes for the bitches. What's more, the owners can't interfere. If you try to force the issue (something that's quite usual in many breeds) they go off the whole idea altogether.

I wasn't going to the pub. I'd come a long way and if I was going to have to pay a substantial stud fee, I wanted to be sure a mating had taken place. Not all matings are productive, of course, but there certainly won't be puppies without one.

We got no mating at all. That particular dog was never successfully used at stud which was a pity because he was a very good specimen.

Other dogs were imported and Aninrak had four litters all told. Her last litter illustrates the sort of thing that can go wrong, and this involves another major dog-breeding cost — the vet.

Diagnostic Disasters ————————

Not long after that episode, I moved to a country town where there were two veterinary practices. Unusually, local dog-breeders seemed vague about which was the better, the only firm statement I was able to get being to the effect that one of them wasn't really interested in small animals. Fair enough: in those days the profession hadn't latched on to the fact that small animals had an extremely lucrative potential and there were practices which didn't want to know. So, when Aninrak was having her fourth and last litter of puppies and had uterine inertia, I called in the other practice.

Uterine inertia is not unusual. It is a condition in which the muscles of the uterus cease working. The cause may be old age, exhaustion after a long labour, or pure laziness. The result can be dead puppies and possibly the loss of the bitch, too. It is customary for the vet to examine the bitch internally to make sure that the puppy about to be born is correctly presented (if it isn't, a caesarian section may be necessary) and then administer a substance such as pituitrin which forces the muscles to contract and expel the puppy. A sensible breeder makes a note of the onset of labour and if no puppies have arrived within two hours, or if two hours have elapsed since the last one, they contact the vet.

The vet arrived promptly enough and agreed that it was uterine inertia but he refused point-blank to give her pituitrin because he 'didn't believe in it'.

'How can you not believe in something as well-tried as pituitrin?' I asked.

'It's far too drastic.' Instead he gave her an injection that he said was glucose and a sedative, which I would have thought was the last thing you gave to a bitch who was meant to be working hard to give birth.

'It will calm her down,' he told me, unperturbed by the fact that she was already calm to the point of placid. 'If she hasn't had them by ten o'clock tonight, give me a ring.' It was five. Another five hours seemed a long time.

By ten o'clock she had done nothing. Again he came out promptly and this time his diagnosis was that she was full of dead and putrefying puppies and would need a caesar.

I stood up. 'I'll call a taxi and get right round to the surgery.'

'No need,' he assured me. 'We'll do it in the morning. Bring her in about eight.'

'But if she needs a caesar, she needs it now,' I protested. 'If you leave it till the morning, she could be dead.'

'I'll give her some antibiotics. She'll be all right.'

By the time he left, any confidence I had in his ability had evaporated and I was very concerned for the bitch's welfare. I also had the great disadvantage of not having a car and therefore being very restricted in seeking a second opinion. I did the only thing I could: I telephoned a vet some thirty miles away who had given the young Alaskan Malamute Club, of which I was Secretary, some excellent advice. Professional ethics raised a number of hazards but he was a subtle man and steered his way carefully round them. He agreed that it was very unusual to delay ten hours before performing a caesarian section but that 'the vet on the ground' may well have had good reason to do so (though I noticed that he didn't volunteer what might have constituted such a reason). He advised me to insist on staying to watch the operation in order to ensure that the anaesthetic she was given wasn't one which would guarantee dead, if not putrefying, puppies. He gave me a list of drugs which it would be inadvisable to use.

That was when I learned that an owner has a right to watch any surgery performed on their dog. This is understandably not something the veterinary profession advertises because obviously the last thing a vet wants to cope with is either an owner who passes out at the sight of blood or one who gets emotionally upset when the knife goes in. For the record, although operations on other people's dogs interest me, I do not exercise my right where my own dogs are concerned simply because I know I *am* emotionally attached to them.

I had a camp-bed in the room where Aninrak was supposed to be whelping. Normally in that situation the slightest unrest by the bitch will wake me up. I can only assume that the strain of the preceding hours had taken their toll and I was unaware of anything until about three o'clock in the morning when I was woken up by some loud whimpering. I switched on the light and looked into the whelping box.

Aninrak was suckling two very un-putrefied puppies and a third one lay to one side, dead.

I had a close look at it. Its body was elongated, something which happens to whelps who spend too long in the 'passage' between the womb and the outside world. In addition, one of its ears had been almost chewed off, presumably by its mother in a frantic attempt to resuscitate it.

I was furious. Two puppies had been born despite the veterinary 'treatment' and a third had been lost unnecessarily: there was not then and has never been since, the slightest doubt in my mind that, had the vet given pituitrin, that puppy would have been born alive.

There was one small revenge I could take. It was, as I said, three o'clock in the morning. I telephoned the vet to give him the glad news. After all, if I was the idiot he clearly took me for, that's exactly what he would expect me to do. He was less than delighted but he was courteous. He warned me that, in the circumstances, the puppies were unlikely to last the night and said he would be round in the morning to check that all was well. That man certainly didn't begrudge house-calls.

He expressed surprise that the two puppies were still thriving and pointed to the dead one as justification for his diagnosis. 'I told you they were dead,' he said.

'To be accurate, you told me she was full of dead and putrefying puppies and there's nothing putrefied about that. It wouldn't even be dead if you'd given pituitrin.'

He smiled patronisingly. 'We can't be sure of that. Now, let me examine the bitch.'

As he did so, his face grew grave. 'I'm sorry, Mrs Edmonds,' he said. 'She hasn't finished yet. I'm afraid there are several more to come yet – and they're dead. We're going to have to operate after all.'

'She's behaving as if she's finished,' I said suspiciously.

'That can be very misleading. After all, you can't be sure.'

Which was true enough, so I agreed to take her to the surgery in two hours.

The taxi driver was very obliging and raised no objection to Aninrak and her two puppies which accompanied us in a cardboard box.

The receptionist, herself a vet and wife of the practice's other partner, was off-hand. 'Leave her there,' she said. 'The vet will see to her when he gets back.'

'Oh, no,' I said. 'I'm staying.'

'You could have a long wait. I've no idea when he'll be back.'

'I've got all day,' I assured her. 'Besides, I intend to watch the operation.'

The off-handedness vanished. 'You can't do that.'

'My information is that I can.'

'Operations are very messy.'

'That's all right: I'm not squeamish.'

She closed her little hatch and her blurred outline disappeared from behind the frosted glass. It was the vet – you remember: the one who hadn't got back yet – who came through the door separating the office from the waiting-room.

'Let's have a look at her,' he said and led the way into an examination room. He poked and prodded. 'Do you know, Mrs Edmonds,' he said at last. 'I think she's finished, after all.'

I smiled. It wasn't easy, but I managed it. 'What a good job you found out before you gave her a twenty-guinea scar,' I said.

The inference cannot have been lost on him but he wisely ignored it. 'The thing is, she's more relaxed here than she was at home. It's easier to be sure.'

'Yes, I suppose she would be more relaxed in a completely strange place,' I agreed sweetly.

He was anxious to vindicate himself. 'Of course, these are *very* large puppies, he said. 'Much larger than one would expect. That can confuse the issue, you know.'

I shook my head. 'They're not larger than one would expect,' I told him. 'I've weighed them and they're a pound and a quarter each. That's about average.'

He ignored that rebuttal and told me instead what a very

sweet-natured bitch Aninrak was. 'So different from most of that breed that we get in here.'

Now there were at that time about thirty Malamutes in England and as Club Secretary, I knew where they all were. None was, or ever had been, anywhere near this area, and I told him so.

I didn't think they'd have the gall, in the circumstances, to send in a bill, but I over-estimated their professional delicacy. When it came, I paid it but my accompanying letter informed them that I should not be requiring their services again and that I would be unable to recommend them to anyone who bought puppies from me. I said I was sure they would be happy to learn that the dead and putrefying puppies now weighed 28 pounds.

After that I went to the other practice which, while it dealt predominantly with large animals, was by no means dismissive of small. Things trundled along quite satisfactorily for a few years, largely, I suppose, because my animals had nothing other than routine ailments. By the time dear old Aninrak became seriously ill, I had been lulled into a false sense of veterinary security. She was very depressed, off her food and quite simply 'wrong' – that indefinable state that is only ever detectable by someone who lives in daily contact with an animal.

I wasn't very happy when the vet insisted on examining her on a table. Not only did it seem unnecessary with such a large dog, but it wasn't easy to heave 90 pounds of resisting flesh up on to it, even with the vet's help. Aninrak cried out – I realised afterwards it must have been with pain – and the vet promptly put a muzzle on her 'in case she bit'. She had never bitten anyone in her life and no one who knew dogs could have interpreted that cry as a threat. He diagnosed 'a tummy upset', told me not to feed her and gave me some pills with which to dose her.

Now I like to know the whys and wherefores of treatment, whether I'm the subject of it or one of my animals. 'What do they do?' I asked.

'They ought to do the trick,' was the reply.

'I didn't assume you were prescribing something that would make her worse. What exactly are they?'

'Just give them to her.'

She cried out again when she jumped off the table.

Since she wasn't eating, anyway, not feeding her presented no problems, though getting her to take the pills was difficult: normally I wrap pills up in butter and hey, presto! they're gone, but Aninrak wasn't even interested in titbits. As the day progressed she got steadily worse. At tea-time I called out the vet. He agreed that she didn't seem very well but stuck to his diagnosis, changed the pills and said we should see a turn-around 'any minute now'.

We didn't. By nine o'clock that night I had no doubt at all that she was dying: although she was breathing normally, she was lying stretched out and, most ominous sign of all, her tongue was lolling out of the side of her mouth. I rang him again.

Whoever was minding the shop told me he was at a party but if it was an absolute emergency, she was empowered to pass on the number. I figured imminent death was an emergency.

I can't blame him for not being very pleased. He assured me I was panicking unnecessarily and that she would probably be as right as rain in the morning; dogs didn't die from tummy upsets.

Leaving aside the fact that that isn't true, I very much doubted whether his diagnosis was correct, though I had no idea what might be the problem. I insisted that I wanted her seen. I shall always remember his words.

'All right,' he said. 'If it will make *you* happier, I'll come.' The inference was obvious: he was leaving his nice, convivial party because this neurotic pet owner was panicking over a dog with a tummy ache.

He brought a young man with him. Whether this was a trainee vet or his son, I've no idea. It didn't matter very much. Aninrak had died before they got there – and they hadn't hung about.

To give him his due, I don't think I have ever seen a man more stunned. He said he couldn't understand it. His diagnosis must have been wrong and would I allow a post mortem? Since I had been going to insist on one, that suited me very well, and it transpired that Aninrak had had a tumour on the liver which had ruptured.

'If it's any consolation to you,' he said when he telephoned the result, 'she couldn't have been saved.'

'I accept that,' I replied, 'but she could have been saved nearly twenty-four hours of agony.'

'I suppose so, if you look at it like that.'

'I do. It's why I call in a vet.'

However, I accepted that it was a genuine mistake. We all make mistakes from time to time and usually we don't make them twice, so I had no hesitation about remaining with the practice.

I began to have doubts when Shiloh was suddenly stricken.

Shiloh was a long-haired, non-pedigree cat of whom I was particularly fond. He had been one of two but his sister Atlanta, to whom I had never warmed, some years before had tackled an HGV and lost. Shiloh was quite different and when one morning he ate his breakfast as usual and discovered, when he turned to jump back on to the floor that he couldn't move from the waist back, he was understandably terrified. I managed to get him into a basket and rushed him round to the vet.

His diagnosis was instantaneous. 'Meningitis,' he said, without bothering to examine the cat. Maybe he used divine inspiration.

'What, suddenly? One minute he's walking, the next he's paralysed?' I knew nothing about meningitis – or paralysis, for that matter – but it seemed odd to me.

'It depends which form of meningitis. Leave him here and we'll treat him.'

I'm always very loath to leave an animal at the vet's. There are, I know, owners who are so emotionally tied to their animals that it stands a better chance of recovery in the peace and quiet of a cosy kennel away from its fussing owner, but a sick animal is already under great stress and if you add to that the trauma of removing it from the home and the people among whom it feels secure – and you can't explain to the animal that it is a temporary move – many lose the will to live and get steadily worse until they die. Especially cats. It is, of course, a nice little earner for the vet.

I telephoned when I got in from work that afternoon but the

receptionist said I'd have to speak to the vet who was out on his calls. Fair enough.

When I rang towards the end of evening surgery, he was apparently out on an emergency. She would get him to ring me when he got back. No, she couldn't comment on the cat: she was only the receptionist.

I couldn't get hold of him that evening at all but when I rang in the morning, a different receptionist answered the phone. White cat? They didn't have a white cat.

'Are you sure? Would you go and check?'

She returned to the phone after a few minutes. 'No, there's no white cat down there,' she said. 'Shall I get him to ring you when he comes in?'

Needless to say, he didn't. I was in the waiting-room when evening surgery started. He was very apologetic.

'Didn't anyone phone you?' he asked. 'I'm afraid he died the day you brought him in.'

'Died or was put down?' I asked.

'Does it make any difference?'

'Yes, it does. He could have died at home, in familiar surroundings. If he needed to be put down, I could have held him so that it wasn't all strangers. He was terrified enough as it was.'

I honestly don't think he knew what I meant. I should have changed practices after that, but I wasn't going back to number one and I still had no transport so, warily, I stayed.

Bayou was what finished that practice off for me.

I had kept one of Aninrak's 'dead and putrefying' puppies, a very handsome bitch called Zampa. Zampa only had one litter because, after producing the first three normally, she needed a caesar for the remaining four, only one of which survived, to be known initially as Hank Macduff, because according to Shakespeare, Macduff 'was from his mother's womb untimely ripped'. (This apt literary allusion was soon dropped and he went through life as plain Hank.) I kept Hank and I also kept a red-and-white bitch I called Bayou.

All went well until they were about four months old, when Bayou started vomiting. I soon noticed a lump on her tummy that shouldn't be there. Puppies swallow all sorts of undesirable things, including stones, and the first thing to do if one thinks there is an obstruction of that sort is to dose the dog with liquid paraffin. On this occasion there was no great laxative effect and no sign of the obstructive object being passed through but the lump disappeared. Bayou continued to bring up the food she was quite willing to eat and eventually the lump reappeared. I took her to the vet who confirmed my impression that she had swallowed something and advised me to give her liquid paraffin. I explained that I'd already been doing that and it had had no effect.

'Then increase the dose and if she hasn't passed any foreign object by tomorrow, let me know.'

Since my dosage had erred on the side of caution, I didn't quibble with this. Still no foreign object and, when he examined her next day, no lump either. It reappeared during the afternoon and this time, being in the neighbourhood, he dropped in to see her. In typical Malamute fashion, she was delighted to see him, even though, by this time she was distinctly poorly.

'There can't be anything very much wrong,' he said. 'It's odd, though. Lumps don't usually come and go like this. Have you found anything missing that she might have swallowed?'

I shook my head. 'No, nothing. Perhaps she should be X-rayed?'

Now I knew he didn't have X-ray facilities and had to make use of the other practice if an X-ray was needed but it was the puppy that was important and I had resigned myself to a temporary visit to number one. However, he did not share my opinion.

'No need for all that,' he said. 'We both know it's an obstruction. It's just a case of getting it expelled.'

'Wouldn't it be helpful to have some idea what it is?'

'It won't make much difference: either it passes through naturally with a bit of medicinal help or we have to operate.'

This seemed reasonable enough, but I knew she was getting rapidly weaker. 'Perhaps it would be a good idea to operate as soon as possible?' I suggested.

'No need. We'll carry on with the paraffin for the time being.'

After three days of liquid paraffin and food which she couldn't keep down, she was very weak indeed, although she still tried to wag her tail when he examined her.

'I don't know what it is,' he said. 'It looks as if I shall have to open her up and see. I'll take her with me if you like and get on with it straight away.'

'It's a waste of time,' I said. 'She's far too weak to survive the operation.'

'Rubbish. She's still quite bright. Come in to fetch her just before evening surgery. She'll be ready to go home by then.'

She wasn't, of course. She was dead. But at least the come-and-go nature of the obstruction was explained. She had swallowed a pair of tights which presumably she had pulled out of the laundry basket and it was the muscular contractions of the intestine that had resulted in their being sometimes bunched up, and palpable, and at other times spread out and impalpable.

This time when the bill came in, I refused to pay. I had no idea whether an earlier operation would have had a better outcome – the vet had told me he had had to make five separate incisions in the gut to remove the tights, and I have no reason to disbelieve him. I do know, however, that if he hadn't wasted three days relying on liquid paraffin, she would have had enough strength to have a chance. Of course, if a vet has done the work, he's entitled to be paid regardless of the outcome. I pointed this out in the letter that accompanied the bill I returned to him and I added that if he exercised his undoubted right to sue me, I should counter-claim for the puppy which, among other things, was only the second red-and-white Malamute to be born in Britain and therefore had a rarity value over and above that which the breed attracted anyway, and that I was sure the local press would have a field day. I was not surprised to hear no more about it.

I moved to a nearby village and acquired some transport. This left me free to travel and for the next nineteen years I used a practice that was about seventeen miles away with only the occasional hiccup. One of the most amusing involved a male Malamute puppy in whom I could detect no testicles.

A dog with no testicles is infertile and may not be exhibited. His value therefore is minimal and it is important to find out whether they are absent altogether or have simply not yet come down. If they're not there, one finds the puppy a pet home as quickly as possible and curses, particularly if the puppy is in other respects a good one. This was the undoubted pick of the litter.

I booked in, I thought, with the senior partner. Perhaps I hadn't made this clear, but in the event the puppy was examined by the new young assistant.

She turned the puppy over on his back. No, they certainly hadn't come down yet but they were there. Give him another month and if they still hadn't descended he could be given hormones. She seemed to be feeling very high up on his abdomen.

'Exactly where are they?' I asked.

She was perfectly willing to show me and I could, indeed, feel hard tissue under the skin, only it didn't feel the least bit like the small, hard pea-shaped ball I was expecting. She was, however, *very* positive and there was no denying the fact that she had the qualifications and I didn't, but when I took the puppy home, I was still unconvinced.

When I got home, I examined the deficient puppy's brother whom I knew to have been somewhat precocious in that respect. He had two balls in exactly the right place. He also had two lumps of tissue precisely where his brother had had them.

Now I knew it was perfectly possible to have a puppy with no testicles but I'd never heard of one with four and I said as much to the senior partner when I saw him next day, having made quite sure this time that my appointment was with the right person.

'It would certainly be worth writing up,' he said.

He felt and prodded and could find nothing.

'Not even up here?' I asked, directing him to the two broad, flat lumps his assistant had indicated.

'Don't be silly,' he said. 'That's mammary tissue. What idiot told you this dog had two up there?'

'Your assistant,' I said. 'Perhaps you would explain to her the difference it makes to the dog's value and the fact that, if I hadn't double-checked, I might well have sold him in all good faith to the immense disappointment of his buyer who would never have believed my story. Neither would his vet. It wouldn't do much for my reputation.'

Better Practice ————————————————

I've given an idea of some of the things that stand in the way of making a fortune out of breeding dogs – or, indeed, any other livestock. It's unfortunate that all the cases I've cited have been tragic. In my more angry moments, I've been known to threaten to become extremely rich by offering some vets an undertaking *not* to publish a book called *Vets I Have Known*. And I wasn't using the verb in its Biblical sense.

Vets don't always make mistakes; they have their successes as well, so perhaps I'd better redress the balance. Mind you, don't forget that even when your dog-keeping activities result in successful veterinary treatment, it still costs money, though perhaps paying the bill hurts less. I'd also better acknowledge – with my tail appropriately between my legs – that the breeder isn't always right, either ...

At the inner-city school where I taught for several years I used to run an annual pet show, judged by a local animal-welfare campaigner on a basis of general condition coupled with each child's knowledge of the care needed by its particular pet. Dogs were banned because I doubted the pupils' ability to stop the bigger ones eating rabbits, guinea-pigs and cats, not all of which had secure containers. At one such show a litter of very pretty black-and-white kittens was entered, with an additional request that I should sex them. This I did and, knowing how difficult it would be to place any females, I said I'd have the only female when she was a bit older.

In the fullness of time Lucy was brought to me and settled in to country living somewhat uneasily. Inner-city born and bred, there were times when we considered offering her to the police for seek and attack work. She duffed up dogs and cats alike if they so much as looked at her. When she was nine months old, I booked her into the vet to be spayed.

He hadn't seen her since she'd had her injections and examined her carefully since he naturally would not perform a non-urgent operation on anything but a fit animal. He glanced up.

'So you've booked her in for spaying?'

'That's right.'

'Well, perhaps you'd tell me how I'm expected to do the operation.'

I was more than a little taken aback. 'How should I know?' I said. 'All I know is that when I pick her up, she'll have an inch-long seam on one side of her abdomen.'

'Then perhaps you'd examine her yourself and tell me what would be the use of that.'

There was a certain something in his tone. I looked. Lucy was male. Very. I hadn't bothered to check when she was brought to me and by sheer chance had never needed to notice since. So she was castrated forthwith and I can't begrudge the vet his comments, most of which hinged on the fact that at that time I'd been breeding pedigree cats for several years. Lucy remained Lucy and, while castration worked wonders for his aggression, I still have a problem with the personal pronoun.

One of the things I liked about that practice was their refusal to give up on an animal too soon. Lucy was one of the beneficiaries of this.

I had been to a dog show in Edinburgh. This had entailed travelling the previous day, staying at a motel that night, continuing to the show, exhibiting, and driving back again on the following day, a schedule aggravated by the fact that I was very anxious to reach home in time to watch Act I of *Siegfried*. I had taken the ever-ebullient Kash with me and the truth behind this story is that I was really much too tired to be sufficiently careful. Once the car was in the garage and the gates were shut, I opened the back and let him out. It was dark and I made no attempt to check that the drive and front garden were clear of hazards.

Now Kash had always had a very great interest in Lucy. Born and bred in kennels, he had never been a house-dog, although he loved being indoors and behaved very well when he was. I always brought him in to wash his white parts and this was where he had encountered the cat, who always kept well away from the kennel area. It would be quite unreasonable to expect a kennelled dog to be safe with cats and neither Lucy nor I were under any illusions about this. However, Kash appeared to have an unwritten rule: he didn't chase (and in Kash's case chase meant kill) unless the object of his attentions moved – and preferably ran.

I haven't the slightest idea how Lucy realised this, but have no doubt at all that he did. When Kash came into the kitchen, Lucy would stay where he was, be it chair, work-top, table or window-sill, very firmly Asleep. Kash would prowl round peering as closely as he could reach, breathing heavily while Lucy appeared oblivious to his interest. Then – and particularly if Lucy happened to be on a chair – Kash would reach over and try to stir the cat up by nudging him with his muzzle. Lucy determinedly refused to react, remaining curled up, his eyes gritted shut. Eventually Kash would give up, partly out of boredom and partly because my ministrations forced him to concentrate on something else.

It was therefore singularly unfortunate that Lucy happened to be in the front garden when I let Kash out of the car. Kash saw the cat before I did and Lucy was too slow on the uptake for his own good. Almost before I could yell, he had bounded after Lucy, who didn't quite make the wall into next door's garden. Kash had him by the loins.

I grabbed the dog by his collar and screamed at him to drop the cat (he knew the order 'drop it') and when there wasn't instant response, I hit him hard and tried levering his mouth open. One of the nice things about Malamutes is that they don't turn on people – a dog of most other breeds would have bitten me by this time. Lucy had no such inhibitions, however, and in sheer terror sank both his teeth and claws into my legs. I secured the cat's release at last and, while Lucy charged, panic-stricken, round the garden, I tried to drag Kash up the steps to the back garden and his kennel.

All this took much less time to happen than it has to retail and at this stage my son, roused by the hullabaloo, came to the door to see what it was all about. Having been brought up always to close doors and gates as soon as he was through them, he closed the front door as I screamed at him to let the cat in, a scream which coincided with Lucy's spotting the open door and making a dive for it, but too late.

By this time, I was half-way up the fourteen concrete steps, dragging with me some 95 pounds of dog who wanted to stay where he was. The sight of the cat diving for the door was too much for Kash who took a flying leap off the side of the steps, dragging me with him. I fell face down in the gravel of the drive. By the time I hit the ground, I had of necessity let go of the collar and Kash had once more seized Lucy. But there were two of us this time. I was handicapped by the fact that one lens of my glasses had apparently smashed and blood was trickling down my face. Once again we managed to free Lucy. My son took the dog up to his kennel and as soon as the door was open the cat fled inside and took refuge under the bathroom radiator.

The continued commotion brought out my neighbours who took me into their kitchen and cleaned me up. When I returned home, I sought out the cat and peered at him. He was understandably in a state of shock and, I knew, needed veterinary treatment on that score alone. But my son doesn't drive and I was in no state to do so, even if I could have seen where I was going. I turned the central heating up and covered the cat with warm blankets. For the time being, that would have to do.

Lucy's back end was paralysed. Unlike Shiloh, who had been panic-stricken, Lucy was too depressed and shocked to react to the situation. He was also too depressed and shocked to eat or drink and he resisted attempts to get a solution of glucose and water into him. My only spare glasses were a pair that were insufficiently strong to risk driving in but my son found the missing lens on the drive, happily not smashed (which says something about its thickness), and had it replaced in the frame. Now I could drive.

The vet confirmed that there seemed to be no internal injuries and gave a steroid injection in order to relieve the pressure and, hopefully, the paralysis. Food, of course, had to be got into him in some form or other.

Now that I knew there were no internal injuries, I had no hesitation in transferring him to a cosy box. I left him in the bathroom, though: it was a warm room, no other animals ever went in it and people only rarely, so it was ideal for his recuperation. From time to time, I succeeded in getting a little substance into him but it wasn't enough and there was no sign of any improvement, as I sadly reported to the vet when we went back.

He had taken Lucy out of the basket to examine him and now the cat lay listlessly on the surgery table. There was absolutely no reaction to any stimulus applied behind the loins, not even the slightest flicker of the tail.

'I'm sorry,' the vet said. 'It looks as if it's beaten us. There just is no life there at all.'

I knew that it was inadvisable to go on giving steroids because of their effect on other organs. 'Then I suppose you'd better put him down,' I said.

The vet filled his syringe and turned back to the cat on the table.

As he reached over to raise a vein in Lucy's foreleg, the cat moved. It was too slow a movement to warrant 'suddenly', but it was certainly unexpected. To our mutual amazement, he dragged himself over to the basket – I must stress that he was still paralysed – gripped the rim and hauled himself up by his front legs and flopped down inside, his useless rear end tumbling over in its turn.

The vet and I stared at each other, temporarily speechless. He emptied the syringe into the sink. 'I think we go on, don't you?'

We did. If there was interest in life, it was worth the risk attached to continuing the steroids, at least for the time being and I'm happy to say that Lucy, his interest in life so unexpectedly restored, made gradual, if very slow, progress. For a long time he was unable to jump at all and still, several years later, doesn't jump as well or as easily as other cats. He can usually make the kitchen table from the ground, but not always. He is also very much more timid and reluctant to step out of doors. I can't blame him for that. He prefers only to go outside when there are no other animals out but there are three dogs whose company he doesn't mind: the Chow, who ignores him completely, a very small German Spitz bitch who is a third his size and as timid as he is, and an elderly German Spitz bitch who bounces at him, but only in a half-hearted way. I sometimes wonder if he has any idea how narrow an escape he had.

Hank, too, had a narrow escape, though in his case the situation was much closer to Shiloh's, the cat I mentioned earlier. As a perfectly fit and healthy dog, he was given his dinner, the first dog in the sequence. As I fed the others I heard him cry out once, short and sharp, then again. I immediately returned to him to find him scrabbling around on his front legs while his back ones dragged uselessly behind. Like Shiloh, he was terrified. I rang the vet to say I was bringing him over right away but that was something easier said than done. I knew I couldn't carry him to the car but if I could coax him over there and lift his front half in, I could push the back end in afterwards.

He was too distressed to be coaxed. I asked my neighbour, a farmer, to give me a hand but when he saw the state the dog was in, he was too afraid of being bitten to risk touching him, I rang the vet again to ask whether, in the circumstances, he would come out. In the event, he sent his veterinary nurse with a sedative injection and we were finally able to heave him into the car and get him to the surgery.

There was no obvious explanation of what had happened, though I noticed that meningitis was not mentioned at all, so it was a matter of treating the symptoms, which meant steroids. The vet eventually decided that he must somehow have trapped a nerve in his neck, perhaps by twisting round at an unorthodox angle. Be that as it may, although he calmed down, there was no improvement after three days of treatment. In particular, there was no reaction when his tail – normally carried over his back but now hanging straight down – was pinched.

'In most cases, I'd say there's nothing more we can do,' the vet said. 'In this case . . . I don't know. I've got a feeling we could win. Shall we go on?'

There was, of course, only one answer. We did and, sure enough, he made a partial recovery, certainly enough to enable him to survive many more years. He was never entirely normal again, though. His tail never again went over his back and he preferred carrying one of his hind legs to putting it on the ground. I sighed about this.

'It's a pity.' I told the vet one day. 'He was a show dog.'

'Oh, I don't know,' he replied. 'Use your initiative. Tell the judge it's a special kind of sled-dog bred to carry one leg so that he doesn't have to stop to cock it.'

It was an appealing idea but somehow I didn't think even the most stupid judge was going to fall for it!

Hot Dogs ——————————————

There was a time when, without the help of a very sensible down-to-earth vet, I might well have lost an entire litter. In terms of general management, it always pays to time a litter carefully if you possibly can. A litter born in spring or early summer gets the benefit of the sunshine and you, the breeder, reap the benefit of dry weather – an important consideration if puppies are reared in kennels. Autumn puppies get wet and winter can be a problem: Malamutes aren't affected by the actual cold (or if they are, there's something wrong), but morning and evening feeds are done in the dark and any veterinary emergency may well mean travelling on icy roads or through fog. High summer is not normally a problem in this country, but there are such things as heat-waves.

There is a limit to how far you can time a litter since the bitch comes into season twice a year and not necessarily at the time you would choose. One such bitch was Arla, whose seasons were as regular as clockwork: May and November which meant puppies in July or January. Now that really *is* Hobson's choice. I took a gamble. My reasoning was that, since heat-waves in England are only marginally less rare than hen's teeth, unlike both fog and snow in the Cotswolds where I lived, I plumped for July puppies. Whenever I take a gamble, I lose.

Arla turned out to be a lazy whelper and it took three visits to the vet for pituitrin before the whole litter was whelped. This was more annoying than worrying but she proved, like most Malamutes, to be an excellent mother and she settled down with her eight puppies in the 'den' of the cupboard under the stairs. If this seems an odd place, it isn't: in that particular house it was in the kitchen; it had a tiled floor and a light and because it was snug and dim, bitches felt entirely secure there. Only when their puppies were out and about did I move them outside.

The previous summer had been hot and dry and it seemed unlikely there would be a second in succession. I reckoned without the geenhouse effect. Just about the last thing puppies needed was snugness, as I was to find out.

Now I make a point of weighing my puppies at birth and at twenty-four hour intervals thereafter until they're weaned. The reason is simple: loss of weight or, more often, the failure to gain weight, is the first sign that something isn't right. When the loss is drastic enough, you recognise it as soon as you pick a puppy up, but the scales register it first. This litter began to lose. All of them.

There is a phenomenon dreaded by all breeders which is known as the Fading Puppy Syndrome, in which, no matter what the vet does, the puppies fade away and die, one after the other. I have never had it but it began to look as if my run of luck was over.

I took them to the vet. Everything tied in with fading puppies except for one inconsistency: there wasn't the slightest indication of any respiratory problem. He didn't know what was wrong with them but he had a hunch it wasn't FPS.

With puppies as young as that – they were less than a week old – you can't do much except treat the symptoms. He gave them antibiotics and, because they were dehydrated, gave me Lectade, a rehydration solution, to feed to them at two-hourly intervals *day and night*.

I brought the fold-away bed down to the kitchen, and the alarm clock. At two-hourly intervals I drop fed each puppy with finger-warm solution. It took a good five minutes per puppy: although at that stage they drank no more than a teaspoonful each, it had to be fed slowly because if the fluid is ingested too quickly it can go 'the wrong way' and get into the lungs. You can do your own sums about the amount of sleep I had.

After forty-eight hours I was able to cut it back to three-hourly during the night. The nights were hot as well as the days and I suddenly realised that the 'den', with Arla curled protectively round her puppies, was like an oven. I couldn't separate her, but I moved out the synthetic sheepskin blankets I use so that they were all lying on bare tiles, and I opened the back door so that what air there was could circulate in the kitchen and the 'den'.

By the end of a week they were gaining again and even when they were getting all they needed from Mum, I still offered them the Lectade.

They throve and, happily, that initial set-back wasn't reflected in their later development, those that have been shown, here and abroad, doing very well indeed. Talking it over afterwards, the vet and I came to the conclusion that the explanation must have been the heat, even though they had never been in direct sunlight either outside or through glass. Some newer vets don't like treating symptoms without getting to the bottom of the cause even though, as in this case, treating symptoms is not only all you can do, but has the desired effect.

So you see, breeding dogs isn't all cuddly puppies and pin-money. There's a lot of expense, a great deal of hard work and more than anyone's fair share of heart-ache. The rewards? Well, they're certainly not financial. The greatest reward is seeing dogs you've bred giving immense pleasure to their owners, whether as pets or in the show-ring. Many would scoff and say that's a poor return. Maybe they'd be right but then, dog breeders would be the first to agree that they're more than a little mad.

— 7 —

ALL IN
A NAME

Shakespeare was wrong. A rose by any other name would *not* smell as sweet. It would smell the same but that's an objective matter of chemistry. Whether or not it would smell sweet is an entirely subjective judgement which would certainly be affected by the name. Two examples, neither of them from the world of dogs, will make my point. I have many times offered a clump of lungwort to young colleagues trying to fill a new, raw garden. Invariably they wrinkle their noses and say they don't like the sound of that. If I then say, 'what about a bit of pulmonaria?' they accept with alacrity. In case you don't know, they are one and the same. Similarly if, in offering sherry, you give a choice between sweet and dry, nine out of ten people will opt for the dry because it's regarded as rather common to like sweet sherry. If, on the other hand, the choice is between Bristol Cream (sweet) and Dry Fly (dry), nine out of ten will opt for the former, though whether because they like it or because it's been heavily advertised, I'm not sure. (If you don't believe me, try it a few times.)

Names are terribly important. They convey an image. That's why novelists like me agonise over finding exactly the right name for a character. An Adam is quite different from a Dwayne. I had a colleague whose first-born was lumbered with the name Sigismund because his parents were determined he would be a concert pianist and they saw that as a good name for a member of that profession. Whether he had the talent to go with the name, I've no idea, but I'm sure he grew up cursing them. His sister was called Easter Sunday, only in Spanish, which made it sound better (Domenica Pasquale). A fit of sanity overtook them with the third one, who was simply Suzannah. Most parents wisely avoid giving their children names which are too outrageous, knowing what hell other children can make for them. In naming pets, at least that consideration doesn't have to be allowed for and the imagination can be given a little more freedom.

There are still constraints that should be borne in mind and the most important of these is the fact that sooner or later the owner is going to have to stand in a very public place and call the dog. I cherish the lesson learned by the owner of a German Shepherd puppy. He saw himself as a somewhat macho individual, although that word was not then in use in this country, and he had chosen an Alsatian because of its popularly assumed similarity to the wolf and that's the name he decided to call it – Wolf. Not only would it fit the dog when it was grown up, but it was also a German name (though he gave it the English pronunciation) and therefore appropriate on that count, too.

All went well for a year or so. Wolf grew into a handsome dog, admired by all who saw him and his owner was gratified by the appreciative comments he received on the appositeness of the name he had chosen.

Then one day the milkman left the gate open, an omission which wasn't noticed until Wolf slipped past his owner and bounded down the garden path and through the gate. His owner was not unduly worried. Like most of his breed, Wolf was intelligent and had been well trained. The owner went to the gate and called.

'Wolf! Wolf!'

The dog was happily investigating something and in no undue hurry to return so the owner called a little louder and a little longer, despite the curious grins of passers-by. When the dog came back, which he did very soon afterwards and in the best of good humours, he found that his name had unaccountably been changed to Max. Try it yourself, out loud, and you will see why.

One or two syllables are best if only because anything longer invariably gets shortened and I have to say I prefer non-human names, or at least names that are not immediately obviously human. I have a Basua, for example, named after Basua Makin, a remarkable lady who was governess to Charles I's daughter Elizabeth. This wasn't why I chose it. When I came across it in the course of some research for one of my novels, I thought, 'What a good name for a dog,' and stored it in my mind for future use. It's actually a seventeenth-century corruption of Bathsheba and it illustrates the inadvisability of three syllables: she is almost always called Baz.

When I imported my first Viennese German Spitz, it seemed appropriate to give him the same nickname as another son of that city, Johann Strauss, who was something of a ladies' man as well as a great musician, so the dog became Schani. I can't claim he has any great prowess as a musician but if his sexual appetite is anything like that of his name-sake, I'm jolly glad I wasn't Mrs Strauss.

Yet another of my dogs was given his call-name by his American breeder. She simply used the initials of his pedigree name – Kimiska's Arctic Sea Hawk – to make the excellent name, Kash. When he arrived here, I added my own affix 'of Highnoons', but an additional H made no difference to the pronunciation.

Pedigree dogs have two names. The first is the name under which they are registered at the Kennel Club, the other is their pet name, sometimes referred to as call-name or kennel-name. People often decry pedigree names as being ludicrously fancy but the point is that, in order to avoid confusion in pedigrees, no two pedigree dogs may be registered with the same name. Since there are over a quarter of a million dogs registered at the Kennel Club every year, that poses problems. One way of minimising this is by granting each breeder an affix, a word which they attach to every dog they breed. This allows the rest of the name to be used elsewhere. My own affix is Highnoons, a name I chose partly because its American associations fit an

American breed and partly because it's the name of a house in one of Georgette Heyer's novels – and I'm an avid Georgette Heyer fan. Friends have the affix Jacbar (made up from Jackie and Barrie), another has Chimofloe (the stud-dog's pet name is Chimo and 'floe' has suitably arctic connotations). We can all, if we wish, use the name, Bob: Highnoons Bob, Jacbar Bob, Chimofloe Bob – three different names. If I've bred the dog myself, Kennel Club rules say the affix goes first (Highnoons Bob) but if I've bought the puppy from someone else, perhaps someone without an affix, it has to go at the end: Bob of Highnoons. If I buy Jacbar Bob, I can still add my affix: Jacbar Bob of Highnoons. In practice it would be extremely foolish for two people in the same breed to choose names that differed only in the affix because it would inevitably cause confusion later on when people new to the breed came to write out pedigrees in which those names occurred.

The writing out of pedigrees is a hazardous business. When two Malamutes were imported into England from Spain, their Spanish export pedigrees had so many spelling mistakes relating to their American predecessors that they were almost unrecognisable and the Kennel Club and I spent considerable time finding out what they should have been, so that the record was accurate. To give just one instance, Champion Kajo's Billy's Bady Buttong should have read Champion Kajo's Billy's Baby Bunting. I'm sure spelling mistakes must be creeping in to pedigrees which have Schani in the background: although he was bred in Vienna, his ancestry is Czechoslovakian and names like Onix ze Sychrovskychestraze and Danuta z Brdskychestraze do rather lend themselves to mistakes!

Some breeders seem to name their puppies at random but most have some sort of scheme. It may be a simple alphabetical scheme: all the puppies in the first litter beginning with A, in the second with B and so on. It may involve the repetition of one word after the affix: Dark Stranger, Dark Night, Dark 'n' Handsome. Some kennels like alliterative names: my Chow was bred by a famous kennel which used only names that alliterated with the affix, Tanlap: Tanlap Tidy Target, Tanlap Tristar, Tanlap Trademark. Others use themes from literature – characters from Tolkien, for example, or from music. The permutations are endless. For my Malamutes I work through the alphabet but limiting myself to names of Indian tribes or famous American Indians. This has produced its own problems because it isn't always possible to find enough names beginning with a particular letter to cover a whole litter, and sometimes I don't like the names there are: I was not prepared to call a puppy Highnoons Flathead, for instance. This, coupled with the fact that some tribal names are other people's affixes means that I have had to miss out some letters of the alphabet altogether, but on the whole it works quite well, even if some people have difficulty pronouncing the names. . . . In my other breed I share a different affix, Dovetrees, with a friend and we each use a different naming policy. I simply go through the alphabet, while she uses themes. To be truthful, thinking up names is almost as much fun as breeding the puppies in the first place.

In the pedigree world, at least in Britain, it has never been considered quite The Thing to choose a pet name which echoes the registered one, the theory being that its use in the show ring could be a not-so-subtle way of telling the judge which dog it was and thereby possibly influencing his verdict, particularly if the dog happened to have done a lot of winning in the past. I think it's a somewhat tenuous argument, since any judge who really knows the breed will recognise the dog without any help, and it is totally disregarded in many countries, especially in America, where winning is all that really matters. Thus, my bitch Dovetrees Christmas Carol, known over here as Teazle, would in the States be known as Carol or perhaps Chrissy. Sadly, the attitude here is changing and with it the practice. Mind you, it can work in reverse. My friend and I bought a puppy from Austria. He hadn't yet been registered and we had to think up a name for the import licence. With every intention of changing it later on, we put down Fritzi, the name which therefore appeared on the documents that went out to the breeder. When his registration papers arrived, he was down as Fritzi von Cottas. As it happened, Fritzi suited him, so it stuck, which was rather a pity since, given the choice,

we'd have preferred a 'proper' name that didn't incorporate his call-name.

A non-doggy visitor once said to me, in genuine amazement, 'Do *all* your dogs have names?'

I was equally amazed. 'Of course they do,' I replied.

'But why?'

Now that took some thinking about, not because I didn't know, but because I wasn't sure how to explain to someone who had needed to ask the question. I countered with a question of my own. 'Don't your children each have a name?'

'Yes, of course, but that's different. They're not dogs.'

'But why do they have names?'

He thought about it. 'For when we want one and not another one, I suppose.

'Exactly. Why should dogs be any different? Sometimes I want Teazle and sometimes I want Zampa. The name tells them which should come.'

He smiled – rather patronisingly, I thought. 'You don't fondly imagine they know which one you mean, do you? It's pure luck if the right one comes.'

'Is it pure luck if the right child comes?' I asked.

'No, of course not, but then, they're intelligent.'

As a matter of fact they weren't, but this was no time to be offensive. I could only assure him that each dog not only knew its name but had learned it within twenty-four hours of its being allocated. I shouldn't have added that last bit. He could just about accept that maybe, just maybe, some dogs *could* learn a name, but that it could do so within twenty-four hours? He wasn't that gullible.

Give a Dog a Bad Name ————————

I've already said that I don't much like human names for dogs. I feel bound to admit that I seem to be in a minority, though someone once complimented me on finding unusual names and said she wished she could do so, so maybe it's lack of imagination. In some breeds there are traditional names. Collies, for instance, have had short sharp names like Toss, Jess, Moss and Fly, for generations, while hounds have a wealth of traditional names to call on, among them Agile, Buxom and Dawdle. Pets of popular breeds are as subject to changing fashions as the names in the birth columns of newspapers. Some – Gemma is a case in point – are very good names for dogs, but they do get a bit tedious when attached to every other pet dog one meets.

Townies who decide to move into the country, buying a biggish house with a fair-sized garden, seem invariably to acquire at the same time two dogs. One will be a Jack Russell, the other either a Labrador or a Golden Retriever. These dogs will be named Ben and Sally. I think they're bought in a job lot with the Arran sweaters, the green wellies and the Barbours. Oh, yes – and the cleft walking stick. Now I do have a tendency to open my mouth and put my foot well and truly in it. One such occasion was when my brother, who happens to be called Ben, rang me up to tell me he was engaged. His fiancée's name was, incredibly, Sally. Without stopping to think, I roared with laughter.

'Is she a Labrador?' I asked.

He was not amused. In fact, the atmosphere between us was a little strained for some time.

The names people choose for their dogs tell you quite a lot about the people, drawing attention to other things besides their lack of originality.

The man who calls his Rottweiler Gnasher, Mauler or Ripper is saying more about himself than about his dog, while the man who calls it Magnum is saying the same thing but with greater subtlety. Mind you, the same names applied to a Chihuahua are simply amusing.

An elderly couple bred a litter in one of the small companion breeds. They decided to keep the two bitch puppies. They called them Pamela-Jane and Wendy. You will not be surprised to learn that they had no children.

Sometimes dogs have names one would never have thought of in a million years, names which are both original and apposite, if not always entirely flattering. Two such which spring to mind are Floormop and Tow-rag. In a similar category came one which surprised me because it wasn't the sort of thing I would ever have expected that owner to choose. Dearest.

The dog in question was a Chinese Crested – a breed with no hair except for a tuft on top of its head, another on the end of its tail and little fur boots on each foot – and at first I thought the word was simply an endearment.

'Do get down, dearest,' was said on one occasion. 'I wish you wouldn't do that, dearest,' on another.

Curiosity got the better of me. 'Do you always use endearments when they're doing something they shouldn't,' I asked.

The owner chuckled. 'Dearest is her name,' she said.

'Really?' I said, surprised. 'It's not the sort of name I usually associate with you.'

'The explanation's quite simple: she's the dearest dog I've ever bought.'

Sounds reasonable to me.

There are two allegedly traditional names that I've never encountered. I've never come across a Rover and the only Fido I ever knew was a cat, though admittedly a cat with something of an identity crisis. He was the only cat I knew who was regularly chased away from his own garden by the birds who used it.

A Household Name ————————

Teazle isn't a bad name, but it caused one of my neighbours some confusion. I have a German Spitz called that and you need to know that Teazle is quite a character. She's eleven years old and I seem to have spent most of those eleven years reprimanding her for one thing or another.

For a start, she has an irritating propensity for barking which I've never been able to curb. There was a blissful three weeks when she was recovering from broken ribs and a punctured lung which meant it hurt too much to bark, but unfortunately – at least, in that respect – she made a full recovery. She has some funny little habits. If, for instance, she finds something which she has a shrewd idea will be taken away from her, she will pick it up and *tiptoe* out of the room with it. It is so deliberately unobtrusive a movement that whenever we see her doing it, we investigate to see what she has in her mouth – close investigation is often needed because she conceals small items in her cheeks, like a hamster, until she can get at them undisturbed.

Other habits are more irritating. No matter what time of day or night, no matter how bad the weather, Teazle has to be the last dog in. She bustles about the garden pretending to be busy but with one eye firmly fixed on the other dogs, and not until the last one is indoors will she follow – usually at a rate of knots designed to indicate that she was only waiting for the door to be opened. When I acquired a Smooth Chow, Teazle had a problem because he, too, liked to be the last one in. He wasn't as subtle as she, merely hanging around the door until the others were inside, and if the weather was particularly bad, he didn't stand by his principles. They did eventually work out a compromise whereby they went through the door together but this never came into operation until there had been some jockeying for lastship first.

Another of her irritating habits is also connected with the business of coming back indoors. The principal reason for putting a dog into the garden in the first place is so that it may spend a penny, and Teazle is extremely good at asking (though admittedly usually just after I've settled myself on the sofa in front of the fire and the television). It's coming back in that's the problem and in this, too, dreadful weather makes no difference at all. She rarely actually asks to come back in but it makes no difference if she does: the ritual remains the same. When I open the door, she's usually right outside it or standing quite close.

'Indoors,' I say. It's a word she understands perfectly well.

She looks at me briefly and then a thought strikes her. 'Hang on a moment,' her body-language seems to say. 'I really must spend a quick penny. Shan't be a mo,' and off she trots, possibly to the end of the garden. There she squats, squeezes out two small drops and comes galloping back, her whole expression saying, 'Oh, God, what a relief; I needed that.'

Needless to say, the word 'Teazle' uttered in varying degrees of impatience is one not infrequently heard in the village. One day, many years after these little rituals had evolved, my neighbour asked me if all my dogs were called Teazle.

I was puzzled. She wasn't a stupid woman and had a couple of dogs herself. 'No, of course not. Only the one. Why would several of them have the same name?'

'That's what I wondered,' she said. 'It didn't seem very sensible but "Teazle" is the only name anyone ever hears you calling.'

By Any Other Name ————————————

My mother had had an elderly friend who had had a succession of dogs in her life. All of them had been Fox Terriers and all had been called Bob. Their photos adorned the main staircase of her very large house. When I was a child, I asked her why they had all had the same name. Her answer was simplicity itself.

'Because I can't be bothered to think of something new each time,' she said.

I'm deeply superstitious where names are concerned. I very rarely use a name twice for fear of condemning the second dog to whatever struck down the first. When I have done, such names have usually been in prior use only a short time, not long enough for the dog concerned to have established itself as a personality. I have usually regretted doing it because, at the very least, one seems to acquire a preconception about what the dog will be like.

No two dogs are the same. Even if they are similar to look at, their character will be quite different. I am always concerned when I meet people who, having just lost a much-loved pet, are hunting for an exact replica to take its place because I know that, even if they find a dog that looks the same − easier in some breeds than in others − it will prove a disappointment because it won't be the same in any other respect. My advice to such people is to get another dog that looks as different as possible because then they won't expect it to be the same, and the memory of the one they've lost will stay intact in their hearts. Such people also forget the vast difference there is bound to be between the elderly companion they've just lost and the energetic puppy with whom they hope to replace it.

Ideally − and I accept that it isn't always possible − the most satisfactory solution is to accept the advancing years and find your 'replacement' before that ageing companion is too old or too ill to be expected to accept a new puppy. Nine times out of ten, the new puppy will give him a renewed lease of life and when the end comes, as come it inevitably will, the second dog will already have dug himself a little hole in your heart. You won't grieve any the less for the older dog, but you will already have become attached to the younger one and you won't be able to fall into the trap of expecting him to be the same – a trap that can only result in disappointment.

On one occasion I was contacted by a couple who had just lost their elderly Malamute and wanted a replacement puppy. Their dead pet had been fourteen years old and the couple were themselves no longer young. I had grave doubts as to whether the puppy was really the best thing for them and when I heard of a young adult dog looking for a new home – through no fault of his own, I may say – I suggested that he might be suitable. The wife, who it later transpired had really wanted a Border Collie (another breed which is far from ideal for older owners), agreed because her husband wanted it, but the arrangement was on the express understanding that I would take the dog if things didn't work out.

The dog started out with the great disadvantage of being considerably bigger than their bitch and by being neither the same colour nor the same markings. In short, he wasn't a true replacement. With hindsight, I recognise that the warning signs were there from the very first phone call I had to tell me they had collected the dog and were delighted with him. Throughout the call they referred to the dog as 'It'. His name wasn't used once and nor was he referred to as 'He'. I brushed this aside on the grounds that they had only just lost a bitch and had fourteen years of 'She' to get out of their system.

As the months passed and I had regular telephoned progress reports, I became increasingly concerned that, despite the fact that the husband – it was always he who called – professed to be very happy with the dog, he still referred to him as 'It' and never, ever by his name, which was Khan.

'It prefers sleeping in the hall.'

'It does enjoy going for its walk.'

'It's very affectionate.'

If words were to be believed, the affection was returned – but not, apparently, to a sufficient extent to use a name, or even the correct pronoun. Always the impersonal 'It'. Something was wrong but I could glean no inkling of what.

Then, after Khan had been there for nearly a year, I had an understandably desperate phone call from the wife. 'It' had attacked and killed next door's Pekinese. The wife's story was that It had broken down the fence in order to get the little dog. The husband's – later – was that the milkman had left the gate open. I've no idea where the truth lies. The neighbours had said that if they replaced the Peke and got rid of It, they would take no further action such as reporting It as a dangerous dog. Which, considering that the neighbours must have been shattered, was extremely forbearing of them.

At this stage, the husband was too upset to speak to me himself, being terribly attached to It. There was of course no question but that I would have the dog. To this day I don't know the truth of what happened. It's a sad fact that when people decide to get rid of a dog, they very rarely tell you the full story, perhaps because they're afraid you won't take it. I don't doubt that It had killed the Pekinese, which was bad enough, but I suspect there may have been more to it than that. All I know for sure is that within two days they had their Border Collie puppy, and that at some stage in the past few months It had acquired a deep-seated dislike of men and had learned just how to use his size to frighten new acquaintances.

Khan was a very dominant dog – what psychologists call an alpha male. Alpha males are found in all breeds, large and small, but large ones have an advantage in dominating people because it's easier for them to make eye contact. Never, ever look a dog straight in the eye. A submissive dog will break the contact because you're already the boss. A dominant dog may attack because you're challenging his dominance. If a dog tries to make you stare him in the eye, it's because he wants to prove to you that he's the stronger of the two. You *must* break the eye contact and then assert *your* dominance by, for instance, making him sit on command (a position from which attack is very difficult). If a dog – especially a big dog – attacks you, you won't win, so you must never accept *his* challenge, always make him submit to yours.

Khan's technique was to come very close – and stare. Although non-doggy people may not understand the significance of this, they nonetheless feel uneasy, disconcerted. They become apprehensive and draw back without realising it. But being human, they retain eye contact because that's what people – well, the British – are brought up to do. Those two unconscious actions tell the alpha male he holds the advantage. The growl follows – if you're lucky . . .

This was the lesson Khan had learned, and Khan is very, very big.

Fortunately I got his measure very quickly and made no attempt to be friends with him. For two weeks I ignored him. I fed him, cleaned him out, took him for walks but the only remarks I addressed to him were orders – 'Heel.' 'Sit.' – I turned my back on him as much as I could and especially when putting his food-bowl down or picking it up, and I never, ever looked him in the eye. To northern Europeans, steady eye contact is supposed to be a sign of honesty and courage. In many other civilisations it is regarded as simply rude. To a dominant dog it is a challenge. That was not a message I wished to convey.

Khan didn't like being ignored. It threw him psychologically to evoke neither affection nor fear. By the end of a fortnight he was desperate to be friends, nudging me into paying him some attention, however small. I finally established myself as his pack leader inadvertently. I had taken him into Somerset on a research trip. I needed a dog because I was going to a very isolated spot, and I decided he needed a change of scene. As I belted down the M5, he suddenly decided it was his turn to drive. Or perhaps he just wanted to sit on my lap. At all events, this great lumbering figure clambering over from the back – something none of my other dogs ever did – took me by so much surprise, to say nothing of the alarm at the potential road accident that was bound to ensue, that it never even crossed my mind that it might be unwise to scream, shout, swear, and clobber him as hard as I could on any part of him I could reach. He retreated in amazement and has never tried it again. He's been with me now for five and a half years – and I wouldn't part with him. He is never, of course, referred to as 'It'.

Khan is fundamentally a sweet-natured dog like most of his breed, and I had a litter of puppies from him before having him castrated. The reason for the operation was that I knew I wouldn't want to use him again and he was a pain – a very noisy pain – whenever the bitch he lived with was in season. This way he could stay with her. They say castration makes dogs less aggressive. I can't truthfully say that Khan wouldn't still kill a Pekinese – or anything else – if he got the chance, but over a period of months he changed completely towards people. He no longer feels the need to prove he's the alpha male. At least, not in daylight. At night he comes as close to being a good guard dog as any Malamute ever does. He's the one who comes with me when I have to drive somewhere at night and I certainly wouldn't recommend a stranger to make eye contact with him in that situation.

All this has digressed somewhat from the importance of names and the impression they create, so I'll leave you with this delight.

I was walking Aninrak through the estate where I lived. It wasn't at all unusual to be stopped by admiring passers-by with questions about her so I wasn't the least surprised when a man paused in front of me.

'What a beautiful dog,' he said.

I agreed modestly that she was, indeed.

'I don't think I've ever seen one like that,' he went. 'What breed is it?'

'An Alaskan Malamute.'

'A what?'

I repeated it.

'Good God,' he exclaimed. 'It sounds more like a disease than a dog!'

— 8 —

RED FACES
ALL ROUND

Dogs can get you into any number of situations which range from the merely awkward to the downright embarrassing. Sometimes the embarrassment arises out of a misunderstanding which itself comes about because not everyone uses language in quite the same way.

When you import a dog, you can visit it more or less when you like: the kennels may impose certain restrictions to enable the staff to get on with their work without interruption but otherwise, after the first two weeks, it's up to you. People quarantining a much-loved pet – and these form the majority – usually try to visit at least once a week. When the dog has been imported for show, the need is to ensure that the dog has got to know his new owner before he comes out rather than to sustain an emotional bonding. Weekly visits are still ideal but the quality of the kennels is more important and if they are some distance away, visits may have to be less frequent and possibly at irregular intervals.

Kash was quarantined next to two large terriers that were almost certainly Airedales. One day the law of averages decreed that I should be visiting Kash at the same time as their owner was visiting them. We smiled and nodded to each other through the wire. She was playing with her dogs in the restricted space available. I was grooming mine. There aren't many other activities one can do in those circumstances.

Eventually the other owner came over to the wire and watched me for a few moments.

'Has he been here long?' she asked.

'He's about half-way through,' I replied.

'Ah. Mine are due out next week.'

'I expect you're looking forward to that.'

She came a little closer and glanced warily over her shoulder before lowering her voice. 'Are you entirely satisfied with this place?' she asked.

The question surprised me. 'Yes, very,' I said un-hesitatingly.

'You think they look after them all right?' she persisted.

If her dogs were due out in a week, it struck me that she had left it a little late to have doubts. I had none. 'Very well indeed. I've quarantined dogs here before,' I told her.

She looked back at her dogs. 'These two are brothers, you know.'

'That's nice. They're company for each other.'

'I'm afraid they're going to be very unhappy when they come out.'

'I'm sure you're mistaken. They'll love being able to run about again.'

She shook her head. 'It's not that. You see, they lost their Daddy while they've been in here.'

It dawned on me that here lay the reason behind the original question about whether I was satisfied with the place. Since the terriers were at least middle-aged, Daddy had probably been quite old, possibly too old to survive the added strain of quarantine which he had presumably had to undergo alone because two is the maximum number of dogs that may share.

'I'm sorry to hear that,' I said. 'But I expect he was old enough to have had a good run. They probably don't feel it as much as you do: after all they've been in here together for six months. They probably won't notice.'

There was a very long pause during which she stared at me, her face rigid, assimilating my words. When she spoke, her tone was distinctly frosty.

'I meant my husband had died,' she said.

What could I say?

A Star is Born ———————————

When Aninrak's first litter was ten weeks old, I was asked to take one of them up to London to appear in the children's programme, *Blue Peter*. My recollection is that they were working their way through a canine alphabet and wanted a husky. In those days there were no Siberian Huskies in the country and the word 'husky' was more correctly used in its generic sense, as a synonym for 'sled-dog'. There were Eskimo Dogs in the country but no puppies, and they wanted a puppy, so along we trotted. Both rehearsal and transmission went as smoothly as anything can do that depends to some extent on an untrained puppy, but the presenters, producer and crew were quite accustomed to working with animals so there were no great crises.

When we had finished, we all went along to the BBC Club which, so far as I can remember, must have been in a separate building. There was a little hiccup at the door, the doorman insisting that dogs weren't admitted, 'as you very well know, Miss Baxter'. Biddy Baxter was the producer.

She smiled at him with great charm. 'But that's not a dog,' she said. 'If you look closely, you'll see it's a small bear cub and I don't think they're banned.'

He looked her straight in the eye without so much as a glance at the puppy. 'So it is. How silly of me,' he said, and in we went.

I sat with the puppy beside me on one of the bench-seats that ran round the walls. He was by now very full of himself and I wanted him in a position from which he could neither untie shoe-laces nor test stockings to see how far they could be stretched without laddering. Two-thirds of my attention had to be on him which was difficult in a room which seemed to be bursting at the seams with people I'd only previously seen on television, but by alternating him between my lap and the seat, he seemed settled enough.

At the table next to ours were members of the cast of what I think must have been the first British soap opera. It was called *Compact*, the title of the magazine in whose offices it was set and was enormously popular. Most popular of all was the actor, Ronald Allen, who played the magazine's editor (and who was later to repeat that popularity in another soap, *Crossroads*). The attention I paid to the puppy only wavered once, when someone came to tell me my taxi was waiting.

In that split second, the puppy – who at that time was sitting on my lap surveying the people at both tables – achieved something that must have been going through his mind for some time.

He stuck his long muzzle into Ronald Allen's beer and drank it.

There are occasions when one could cheerfully die.

The Television Centre – which was not where *Blue Peter* was filmed – had not long been built at that time and I think still held some kind of mystique for BBC staff. It was said that there had been a notice just inside the main doors, which read: 'Unaccompanied Dogs Not Admitted.' It remained there until someone pointed out to the powers-that-were that there was a certain illogicality about it . . .

Aninrak had quite a comfortable modelling career in her early days, when I was not working and was therefore free to take her about. I found that photographers and advertising agencies had very little understanding of the way a dog's mind works. We went to one studio where the brief was apparently simple. They were photographing an advertisement for a Canadian brand of tinned food that was sold only in Canada. A mock-up of two internal walls of a log-cabin was the basic set. A stuffed moose-head hung on one wall and the human models – mother, father and a child of each sex – were to be clustered round a table laden with canned goodies (though not, of course, clustered in such a way as to obscure any of them. This took some time to arrange). Aninrak's job was to lie on the floor under the moose-head looking alert and interested. This was less easy than it sounds because the lights made it very hot and arranging the humans took a very long time. Consequently the main problem so far as she was concerned was keeping her awake.

There was one other prop and it was a crucial one. In order to add a further touch of Canadian authenticity, and perhaps also to indicate that this statistical family didn't exist solely on a diet of tinned food, there was to be a whole salmon prominently to the fore of the picture.

Everyone agreed that the salmon was essential but it increased the art director's problems: placed on the table, it obscured some of the products, yet placed on the floor, no one would believe the family would then be prepared to eat it. Besides, it could be held to imply that the food wasn't canned in the most hygienic of conditions. Hanging it on the wall, together with a fishing-rod – fishing-rods and shot-guns were present with some liberality – was considered but unfortunately the salmon was very dead indeed and there was a strong probability that it would fall to pieces under its own weight. In the end they laid it along the front of the table and stood the tins on shallow steps behind so that their labels could be clearly seen.

However, it was a long time before someone came up with this solution and in the meantime the salmon was moved from here to there and back again over and over. Every time it was carried past Aninrak, the smell it left in its wake drew her as if she had been attached to it by a thread. It was quite funny to watch: the salmon passed and with one smooth movement she awoke from her stupor, rose to her feet and exhibited every intention of grabbing it. The art director was not amused.

'We've got the dog exactly where we want it,' he snapped after the third pass. 'Can't you keep her there?'

'If you stop waving the salmon in front of her nose, she'll settle down again,' I told him.

He obviously hadn't had the slightest idea that it was the salmon that brought her to her feet. 'What's the salmon got to do with it?' he asked.

'She wants it.'

'What on earth for?'

'To eat.'

'But it's off!'

'All the tastier. The greater the putrefaction, the more willing a dog is to eat something.'

As it happens, this is a proven scientific fact, but he didn't believe it. He stopped shifting the fish about, though, and eventually got his photos. Sadly, Aninrak didn't get the salmon.

That was also the day I came close to losing her.

I rarely went to London so I made the most of the opportunity by going up early to have a look round that most luscious of stores, Harrods. Well, it was luscious in those days, before they filled every available bit of floor-space with merchandise, like a Debenhams or a C&A. In those days, too, the British were pro dogs and you could take them into shops and restaurants (where, as often as not, they would be offered a bone as well as a bowl of water), thus giving the dogs plenty of socialising so that they were accustomed to meeting strangers and learned to take all sorts of unforeseeable little incidents in their stride.

Harrods was unusual in not welcoming dogs in the store itself, but it made up for this by providing a range of kennels in the basement where dogs could be left under the supervision of a doorman. I left Aninrak in his care and spent a pleasant couple of hours browsing among enticing goods.

'I've come for my dog,' I said when I returned. 'The Malamute. The black and white one.'

I was a little surprised when he reappeared with a very large, very grey, Irish Wolfhound.

'No, that's the wrong dog,' I said and edged past him. I could see Aninrak waving her tail expectantly. 'That's mine. The black and white one.'

'But this is the one you brought in, madam,' he insisted.

He was finally convinced, not by anything I said, but by Aninrak's obvious pleasure in seeing me but even as we left the kennels, I had the feeling there was still a doubt in his mind.

— 9 —

BEWARE OF
THE - DINGO?

Not all my dogs have been dogs in the accepted sense of the
word. Digger was a Dingo. Zoologically speaking, Dingoes are
dogs, though opinion is divided as to whether they're wild
animals or the descendants of feral ones. They certainly aren't
conventional pets and pose sufficient problems to make them
generally unsuitable as such.

An acquaintance of mine, also a dog breeder, saw an advertisement in *Exchange and Mart* for a pair of Dingoes and
went to see them out of curiosity. She was so appalled at the
conditions in which they were kept that she promptly bought
both of them.

The Dingoes, as a little thank-you for warm bedding, regular
food, clean quarters and access to fresh air, presented her in the
fullness of time with a litter. Digger was the smallest and I put
him with a Malamute bitch, Gila, and her daughter, Szminka,
who at ten weeks old was the same age as the Dingo.

Like Malamutes, Dingoes howl, only they do it on such a
high pitch that it becomes painful to listen to. Szminka, with
a Malamute's capacity for imitation, acquired a Dingo howl
which she retained to the end of her life, incongruous as it
was on a dog of her size. It was an acquisition I could well
have done without and so, I suspect, could the neighbours.

Digger was for the most part a pleasant, amiable creature, but
not an unalloyed delight. I was asked to take him to an informal

get-together of Spitz breeds called the Spitz Spectacular. Broadly speaking (there are exceptions), the Spitz breeds are those originating mainly from the Arctic and sub-Arctic regions and have small pricked ears, curly tails and a double coat which is usually thick and can be long. They are the breeds which have diverged least from the dogs of early man. Dingoes come into this category and they haven't diverged at all.

Dingoes are hunting dogs and Digger was no exception. At the meeting I sat with him on my knee and chatted to the lady beside me who was interested in German Spitz. Digger was the sort of dog who takes a profound interest in what other dogs are doing and, as we chatted, I was quite pleased that he had got over his desire to leap off my lap and join in. He wasn't sitting still, however, and when I looked down to find out why his front end was wriggling quite determinedly, I saw to my horror that he had my companion's silver fox coat in his mouth and was trying to kill it . . .

Unfortunately he was a confirmed escapologist and if he got out, totally ignored any attempt to call him back. I had to creep up on him when he was immersed in some investigation or other and take him by surprise, for which reason he always wore a collar. He also became quite dangerous if there was a bitch in season on the premises and had no hesitation at those times in setting about with his teeth if there was any attempt to make him do – or stop doing – something he didn't want to do.

The difficulty in getting him back caused a problem when we were involved in a car smash. He was sitting in the back of my van with his lead clipped on to his collar. The purpose of this was to give me something to have hold of whenever I had to open the door because otherwise he would be through it and away.

We skidded in some slurry and hit a stone wall. The wall hit back and, being the stronger of the two, reduced the van to a write-off. The shock of the skid and the impact was such that as I climbed, shaking, out of the wreckage, I completely forgot to grab Digger's lead. He shot past me and into a field bordering a game preserve. I imagine he was pretty shaken, too. I tried to go after him but my legs weren't up to clambering over gates and I had to leave it until the van had been towed away and I had had several cups of tea at home and was thinking straight – well, straightish – again.

The fact that he had a lead on was now a matter of concern. I knew he'd survive in a pheasant-rich environment, but if the lead got tangled in the undergrowth, he might very well starve to death if he didn't strangle himself first. There was also the little matter of the gamekeepers of the three estates which abutted the field where I'd last seen him. He might well seek dinner on any of them. One of these gamekeepers was known to be very trigger-happy where dogs were concerned, which added to the risk.

Now as it happens, it's just a teensy-weensy bit awkward to ring up a gamekeeper and tell him there's a Dingo loose among his pheasants, partridge and guinea fowl and please don't shoot it. So I didn't. I managed to convey the impression I'd lost a sandy-coloured mongrel without actually using that particular noun. I very much doubt if any of them would have been as concerned and helpful as they were if the word 'Dingo' had passed my lips!

Our trigger-happy friend was particularly so, assuring me he distinguished between dogs which were loose accidentally, like Digger, and those whose owners just turned them out because they were too lazy to exercise them properly. He promised not to shoot him, no matter what: he thought they would probably be able to lure it into a loose-box and then they'd send for me.

Naturally, I had no intention of just waiting for them to find him and I didn't delude myself that Digger would be so pleased to see him that he'd come running to his name. Gila was my secret weapon. She came with me.

Not only was Gila his adoptive mother and his live-in companion, she was also in season so they'd been kept apart for some days. I accepted that he might have wandered some way from where he'd escaped but if he was findable, Gila would find him. More accurately, perhaps, he'd home in on an in-season bitch.

I wasn't daft enough to let Gila off her lead – I didn't want to have to hunt for two dogs, thank you very much. We climbed into the field and scoured it pretty well, calling all the time but to no effect. Then we headed for a small copse.

Suddenly Gila's interest sharpened. Her ears were stiffly erect. She had seen something move. We had already glimpsed several rabbits of which she had taken no notice at all, so what was this?

Then I saw it, too. Something sandy-coloured and not very big. This was the time for a risk. I let Gila off the lead.

She bounded away towards the object she'd spotted and there, suddenly, was Digger, obviously thrilled to bits to see his very dear friend and in so interesting a state, too. They left the trees and charged round and round the field. Digger's lead trailing. I let them get on with it. Neither of them was going to take notice of me, anyway. Only when Gila began to tire did I bother to call her. Being a Malamute, she naturally didn't come but she waited politely until I caught up with her and clipped on her lead. I tried to get hold of Digger's by stepping on the trailing end but he was too wily for that and kept just out of reach. Fortunately he had no intention of being parted from his fascinating friend and trotted happily home with her, his lead trailing and one eye watching me in case I swooped.

I don't know whether he caught any pheasants during that little escapade but he certainly knew what to do with chickens. I kept half a dozen Marans in a run on the garden and came home one day to find that he, Gila and Szminka had somehow got out on to the garden and were working as a co-operative – the Malamutes broke down the chicken wire, Digger killed and the Malamutes ate. There were two survivors, a hand-reared cockerel who regularly chased and bit the post-girl, and one hen, and since there was no point in keeping them, I nursed the hen back to health – she had been badly mauled – and then gave them to a local smallholder.

I also swore profusely, but you can't blame dogs – as well as Dingoes – for doing what comes naturally.

A Sad Necessity ————————————

Sometimes, no matter how hard one tries not to, the conscientious dog owner has to decide to put down a perfectly healthy dog because he quite simply isn't safe. Kaiser was a case in point.

Kaiser was another escapologist with tendencies that sadly turned out to be lethal for him before they could become lethal for anyone else. He was an Estrela Mountain Dog and a confirmed escaper.

He was born in quarantine and he and his siblings were the first of the breed ever seen here, which made his eventual loss more serious than it might otherwise have been. The breed was something of an unknown quantity except in so far as they were known to be a guarding breed in their own country, Portugal. They are very handsome dogs, superficially not unlike a brown Pyrenean Mountain Dog but actually a great deal more lightly built and considerably more agile.

I don't recall how old Kaiser was before he discovered he

could sail over the four-foot panels that bordered the front garden but once he had found out how to do it, he wasn't prepared to give up on it. The word 'No!' might just as well not have been uttered.

I did the obvious: I hammered some battens to the fencing panels and stretched small-mesh chicken-wire between them, thereby raising the barrier by two feet. This, I knew, would deter most dogs even though they would walk right through chicken-wire if it were at ground level, and one of my worries was that the Malamutes would follow Kaiser's example since dogs do occasionally learn by imitation.

It worked. For two whole days. Then he discovered a weakness in the batten at one end, leaned his front end on it so that the batten leaned to one side and Kaiser could take off between the rest of the chicken-wire and the side elevation of the cottage next door, against which the batten had been resting.

This time I hammered in a six-foot length of four-by-four – no easy task in a garden composed largely of oolitic limestone under three inches of top-soil. I straightened the batten and nailed it to this. *Beat that,* I thought, and went indoors.

He did, of course. This time he selected a stretch of wire roughly mid-way between two battens and leant his chin on it so that it bent over, then he jumped up and rested his front half on it and then, when it had been flattened sufficiently, he stood back and jumped over.

By this time I was getting desperate. I straightened everything up, hammered in a few more nails and posts, and added a stretch of chicken-wire that sloped inwards over the garden. The principle was the same as that used in fencing off military installations – you can't climb over the over-hang. I hoped he couldn't jump it, either, since the changed perspective would make it more difficult to estimate how far back to stand.

This time it worked. Kaiser made several attempts and failed. Then he discovered that it was much easier to sail over the six-barred iron gates.

Since I am not the World's Greatest Handyman, the front of my property now looked as if Heath Robinson had successfully tendered to make Fort Knox secure. More barricades above the gates, to say nothing of the brick pillars supporting them, which Kaiser hadn't yet discovered, would be too unsightly even for me to tolerate. Kaiser's access would have to be much more restricted. He would only be able to go out there if I had time to be with him.

There was a reason for this beyond the fear of losing him or the undeniable fact that a loose dog is a danger, not only to himself, but to any traffic. Kaiser had begun to exhibit the characteristics that make Estrela Mountain Dogs such efficient guards of their masters' flocks. He was deeply suspicious of anyone who was not a member of the family – with whom, I have to stress, he was never anything but a great big softy – and saw no reason to warn them of his mistrust. It was easily controllable in the house, in my presence. I wasn't so sanguine about what would happen if he met a stranger when he was unsupervised.

My fears were justified one glorious spring day when I was exercising him in a steeply sloping hay-field. It had been grazed down over the winter and now the north-facing slope had burst into life with its covering of cowslips and wild purple orchids. A public footpath rang along the bottom of the slope. Kaiser and I were on the broad, flat stetch at the top.

When a small group of ramblers climbed over the stile that straddled the footpath, I thought nothing of it. Ramblers on fine days were a not uncommon sight and they invariably kept strictly to the right-of-way.

Suddenly Kaiser was gone, a mahogany streak charging headlong down the slope, oblivious to his name. It would be a lie to say I raced after him – if I'd tried, I'd have fallen flat on my face – but I certainly went down that hillside as fast as I safely could. This proved to be not fast enough. I arrived as Kaiser sunk his teeth into the ankle of the one man in the group. Many dogs have an instinctive dislike of men. I hadn't realised Kaiser was among them. Fortunately the rambler was wearing heavy walking-boots and the dog's teeth barely marked them. I grabbed his collar, clipped on the lead and apologised profusely saying, with absolute truth, that he had never done such a thing before.

No-one had been hurt, though I knew that wasn't for the want of trying, and the ramblers were very kind and understanding about it. Looking back, I can only assume that my surprise, horror and regret were so unfeigned as to disarm any recriminations they might otherwise have been (justifiably) inclined to hurl. From then on, Kaiser was exercised on a lead.

His propensity for attack – though not, in this instance, for escape – manifested itself some months later when he bit a policeman, an event which says something not very complimentary about his powers of discrimination.

At that time my job involved travelling all over the county, teaching for a fortnight at a time in each of the county's secondary schools. I usually took a dog with me, partly for company on the often long journeys and partly because many of the schools were sited within easy reach of beautiful country walks in either the Chilterns or the Cotswolds.

On the day in question, I had been at one of the further-flung establishments and Kaiser had kept me company. He was a good traveller and curled up in the back of the van and slept during the journey.

He woke up when we reached a traffic census point and stopped. As I wound the window down to answer the census-taker's questions she leaned forward, the better to be heard.

Immediately, Kaiser was on his feet, growling.

'I wonder if you'd pull your head back a bit,' I suggested. 'I'm afraid he's not very friendly.'

She stepped back sharply and was about to ask her first question when the policeman who always attends these occasions came up. I imagine he must have thought either that I had been rude or unwilling to cooperate. He took her place and pushed his face, not just up to the open window, but in it.

'What seems to be the problem, madam?' he said.

Before I could open my mouth to say, 'No problem,' Kaiser had lunged forward and bitten him on the side of his face. He drew blood.

I think the policeman was more stunned than angry. 'That's a dangerous dog, madam,' he protested, reasonably enough.

'On the contrary,' I said. 'He's doing what he's there for.'

'Indeed? And what might that be?'

It seemed to me that this was one of those occasions when the timid, helpless female might be useful. 'Well, you see, my job involves travelling all over the county and you hear such awful stories these days. I decided it was either a gun in the glove-compartment or a dog in the back, and I thought the dog was probably the more acceptable. His job is to repel boarders. As a matter of fact, I wasn't even sure he'd be any good at it so I'm glad to have it proved.'

'But I'm a policeman, madam!'

'Yes, *I* know that and *you* know that, but *he's* never seen one before. All he saw was a strange man dressed in black.'

It was a plausible argument − and perfectly true, as far as it went. He rubbed his face. 'I think you'd better keep a careful eye on him in future when the car window's down,' he said.

'Oh, I will, Officer,' I assured him and that, by sheer good fortune, was the last I heard of it. The constable would have been perfectly within his rights to make a court-case out of it, and I wouldn't have had a leg to stand on. Kaiser was very lucky.

But some months later, he pushed his luck too far.

It was a warm, sunny day and all the dogs were indoors because I was in the front garden talking with the odd-job man. We had long since stopped discussing whatever it was he had come to see about doing and he was delving into his extensive reminiscences about the village forty, fifty, sixty years before, interspersed with hints on how to house-train pigs and recollected incidents during the Battle of Jutland. Neither of us took much notice of a young mother walking down the hill with a push-chair, her pace geared to that of the toddler at her side.

Kaiser saw them, though, from his vantage point in the landing window.

The first either of us knew of his presence was when he hurled himself out of the open window and landed on his side on the concrete path beneath.

'That'll learn him,' was my first uncharitable reaction.

It didn't, though. Barely winded, he picked himself up, threw himself over the six-barred gate and charged, head down, straight for the toddler.

I don't think I have ever screamed at a dog quite so loudly as I did then. The scream contained his name and the urgency was, thank God, enough to halt him in his tracks for once. His interest was momentarily diverted and by the time he had decided I was mad, I was beside him with a firm grip on his collar.

The mother, oblivious to everything except that scream, looked round, understandably startled.

Somehow I managed a weak smile. 'I'm sorry,' I said. 'Only he slipped out, you see, and he is rather large and I didn't want the little girl frightened.'

I suspect she thought I had gone to rather excessive lengths to prevent it, since she looked rather mystified.

After that, I decided that Kaiser was just too much of a liability and I had him put down. I was strongly criticised for this by other people in the breed, all of whom were quite sure that if I'd given him to them, they would have been able to 'do something about it'. Maybe they could have, maybe not – who knows? What I did know was that, since he was indubitably the best of the males, he would have been used at stud and I could see no merit in risking that temperament being passed on.

I have never had the slightest doubt that I did the right thing, but that doesn't mean the decision was an easy one. As I've said before, Kaiser was a delight within the family and I was very fond of him; I dislike putting down a perfectly healthy young dog – though, as my vet pointed out, it's debatable whether a dog that bites indiscriminately can be described as 'perfectly healthy' in any psychological sense. The simple truth is that Kaiser was dangerous, and I firmly believe that there is no place in today's society for dangerous dogs.

Two by Two ————————————

Khan had a different problem. He wasn't wildly smitten with people, especially men, but he *hated* dogs. Maybe next door's Pekinese used to goad him by yapping from the safety of his side of the fence. Whatever the reason, it was soon clear when I took him for a walk that Khan wasn't safe with other dogs. Controlling his tendencies on a walk – and, by definition, on a lead – raised no great problems. In a multi-dog household the situation was rather different.

If a dog is a member of the family it doesn't matter that it's the only dog – in fact, it's an advantage. It's quite another matter if the dog has to be kennelled. Dogs need the companionship of others. You don't have to be a genius to realise that this is a bit tricky if the dog has Khan's clearly demonstrated propensities. I had no idea what sex next door's Pekinese had been but there was an outside chance Khan would accept a bitch with whom he could then live.

I waited until my son came home for Christmas: it takes two to split up a fight between two big dogs and, having been brought up with Malamutes, he isn't afraid of them, knowing, as he does, that they won't turn on people – a characteristic that makes them different from most breeds. (In all honesty I have to say that I've seen exceptions, but they've always been dogs whose male owners think beating hell out of a dog is the way to control it.)

We decided to wait until after Boxing Day, reasoning that if, as was quite likely, there was any repair work to be done, the vet would prefer it *not* to be over the holiday.

If you are doubtful about introducing one dog to another, they must meet unleashed and on neutral, spacious and well-fenced ground. In this case, the drive.

First I brought down the bitch, Zenta. Then we opened the gates from Khan's run. The Light Brigade had nothing on him. He charged out like a Sherman tank and instead of wasting precious fighting time on the canine courtesies, like sniffing, simply bowled her over and then turned on her.

Initially bewildered, this cavalier treatment made her extremely angry and she set about demonstrating that sheer bulk isn't necessarily an advantage.

We gave them, I suppose, about 30 seconds, though it seemed much longer. Then I nodded to my son and we moved in to split them up before there were signs of blood.

As we stepped forward, Khan made the momentous discovery that Zenta differed from previous enemies. Zenta was female. He stopped in his tracks and sniffed at her as closely as she'd let him which, understandably in the circumstances, wasn't very. His whole manner changed completely. 'Look, I'm awfully sorry,' it said as he circled her, tail waving ingratiatingly. 'It was a mistake, an oversight. I didn't mean it. Really I didn't.'

Zenta sat in the drive as nearly as possible with her legs crossed and kept him at a distance by the simple expedient of snapping at him. There was nothing coy about her attitude. If ever a bitch uttered the royal words 'Naff off', it was Zenta just then.

Satisfied that the danger was passed, we put them both in Khan's run and after an evening during which we heard Zenta telling him at intervals *exactly* what she thought of him, they got on like old friends.

Later on I let her have a litter by him and when she finally went to Australia, I introduced him to his youngest sister, Nari. This time his approach was a great deal more circumspect. He had learned that not *all* dogs deserve the same treatment and nowadays lives with his grand-daughter, Safi, in perfect harmony.

Mind you, even dogs who look for trouble can produce some surprises. Khan's father, Kash, didn't – but neither did he back down from it if it materialised, so he and his son were strictly segregated. When we moved to the Fens, I instituted a system whereby each dog had a day-pen inside a very large, security-fenced run. Each dog spent half the day in his day-pen and the other half in the big run. Later, each was to share the big run with Safi but at the time in question she was still very much a puppy and living in the house.

My son visited for a few days and came in one evening from fetching the coal to ask if I knew that Kash and Khan were together in the big run.

'Don't be silly,' I said. 'Khan's out but Kash is in his day-pen.'

'No he's not. They're both out.'

Quarter-of-a-century's teaching experience contributed to the heavy patience of my voice. 'No he's not. I'm not that silly. It must be an optical illusion. He *looks* as if he's there because the light's bad and you just can't see the wire.'

My son was more than capable of matching my tone. 'Mother, I know what I saw. They were sitting side by side watching me get the coal.'

I shot out of my chair with the speed of a world-class athlete leaving the starting-block.

He was right. I must have failed to close one of the gates properly. There they were, perfectly amicably mooching around the run together. I couldn't believe it. I went indoors and telephoned a couple of friends who knew both dogs well. 'Guess what?' I said.

'I don't believe it,' one said flatly.

'You have to be joking,' was the other's response.

Both added what I knew myself – that it couldn't last.

All the same, it was worth a try, if only because it meant each dog had 'proper' company all day long. That night, and the successive ones, I left them where they were instead of transferring them to their night kennels because to put either in the other's territory would be asking for trouble. The big run, having been used by both of them at some time during each day, was safely neutral. I fed them separately in their day-pens. This was a routine they were used to and food can cause quarrels because dogs have no sense of fair play: if two bowls of food are put down, a dominant dog will want both – and these were both dominant males. I exercised them separately, too. It isn't always realised that even more fights start as two dogs go through a restricted gate-way than ever start over food. Apart from that, they mixed.

For three days.

As those three days progressed, they became visibly more wary, more cautious, less amicable. They kept punctiliously – too punctiliously – out of each other's way. Their body-language became increasingly belligerent. Each dog was stiff-legged, the hair of his ruff swift to be raised. There was the occasional warning growl. On the third day they had a short, sharp set-to.

Now a dog-fight normally continues until one dog submits to the other (we're talking normal dogs here, of course, not fighting breeds.) It does this by rolling (or being forced) onto its back so that the other can sniff at the most vulnerable parts of its body: the throat, abdomen and genitalia. This is a ritual like a child calling 'Pax'. Sometimes the victor will actually hold the vanquished down by a paw on its chest, releasing it only gradually and with accompanying growls, but not actually walking away until its defeated opponent is prepared to remain in the submissive position even when it isn't held there.

This fight didn't last long – indeed, it scarcely merited the name. The dogs were evenly matched for size and dominance. Neither was going voluntarily to submit to the other, neither was going to be able to force the other to submit and, more importantly, they both knew it. So – quite unexpectedly so far as I was concerned – they simply separated.

Each dog was, however, severely depressed (yes, dogs can suffer from clinical depression, too!) by the fact that he hadn't been able to establish dominance over the other and, perhaps more importantly, by the fact that no pecking-order had been settled. In human terms, neither had been deposed but neither knew exactly where he stood in the scheme of things. This meant that there had to be a next time – and a next, and a next until an ultimate victor was in place. There would never again be such a bloodless solution, so we went back to the old routine.

They did, once and by accident, find themselves free on the garden at the same time. Each pretended the other wasn't there. Kash went back to the big run and Khan trotted purposefully into his night kennel. It took a second's hesitation once they had caught sight of each other and another two or three before an encounter was safely avoided. They don't *want* to fight, but they know – and I know – that there comes a time when a dog's gotta do what a dog's gotta do. It's up to me to prevent it.

– 10 –

ON THE SAME WAVELENGTH

The first thing anyone does when they buy a puppy is to give it a name and no-one is surprised to discover that it has learned it in twenty-four hours. This is because bribed dogs learn fastest and there's no bribe as good as food where a dog is concerned. Puppy owners don't think this out, of course – they just use the puppy's name when they feed it, which should be four times a day, and that's all it takes. Maybe the understandable rapidity of this particular piece of learning deludes people into ascribing to their dogs intellectual heights far beyond any dog's capacity.

Everyone knows the little old lady whose dog understands every word she says. People who don't own dogs tend to regard such people as both stupid and besotted. They may be besotted but they're not all that stupid.

Dogs may not have the humanoid intellectual capacity with which they're sometimes credited but they're a lot more astute than many people realise. They pick up things remarkably quickly, especially if they're things you'd rather they didn't pick up, such as the precise significance of the word 'out' and they have what, for want of a better phrase, I will call a sixth sense which enables them to gauge a mood, to pick up intentions, before they've been voiced.

Of course no dog quite literally understands every word anyone says to it. You can stand in front of your much-loved pet until the cows come home lecturing him on the dualism of Wagner or the metaphysical implications of the post-Petrine iconostasis, and it will wag its tail because it likes having your undivided attention, but it won't understand a word. On the other hand, when it comes to everyday matters that are likely to affect it personally, it will be sufficiently quick on the uptake to give the impression of total comprehension.

Among themselves, dogs have an extremely complex communication system which depends almost entirely on body language and they are very quick to learn our own relatively simple and usually unconscious body language.

For example, when you're thinking it's about time you let the dog out, or took it for a walk, you make all sorts of restless movements that the dog quickly learns are the forerunners of the walk itself, and the interpretation of these signals is helped by the fact that you probably make them at more or less the same time every day.

They learn to interpret our body language far more quickly than we learn to interpret theirs. I referred elsewhere to the fact that to a dog, eye contact represents a challenge. Pet dogs learn very quickly that humans regard it as something else – fearlessness, perhaps, but not in an agressive sense. For us it's a sign of integrity that is fearless in the sense that it has no fear of being 'found out' (which is why con men take very good care to look their victims straight in the eye ...) When pet dogs are dealing with their owners – though not usually in dealing with other humans – they will do it themselves, apparently because it gives their owner pleasure. They never make the mistake of trying it on another dog. In a similar way, one of my German Spitz, Teazle, has learned to smile. I don't mean the apparent smile that crosses the face of, say, a Samoyed, by virtue of the construction of its mouth, but a definite muscular drawing-back of the lips to reveal the teeth. It's quite different from a silent snarl and, as a matter of fact, it's rather unattractive. She does it in conjunction with coming very close to me and gazing into my eyes. I know of only one other dog that does it, also a German Spitz that, like Teazle, is very much a pet.

Humans don't make any attempt to understand the signals dogs give out, much less to imitate them. When I was house-hunting in the countryside some distance from Tangier, our presence had a very unsettling effect on one of the local dogs. These dogs wander round the villages but they are not strays. They have homes, though they're not allowed inside them, and they're fed and watered in return for which they act as watch-dogs either around the houses or for the small flocks of sheep at the roadside. This particular dog didn't like us from the moment we got out of the car and followed us as we walked all round the outside of the perimeter wall of the property we had our eye on. He barked a warning the whole time which meant that people in the adjacent houses knew we were there.

I knew, both from the distance the dog kept between him and us and from the whole manner of his barking, but particularly the shape of his lips which were funnelled over his mouth, hiding his teeth, that he had no immediate plans to attack. So I ignored him. My Moroccan companion, however, was seriously alarmed, as was I when I saw him surreptitiously pick up a small rock. His eye was more firmly on the dog than on the property we had come to look at.

'What's that for?' I asked, though I knew the answer.

'The dog. He's too close. He's going to bite.'

'No, he's not. He's keeping his distance. He hasn't got any closer than he was when we arrived.'

'These dogs can get very nasty. They're not like pet European ones.'

'You'd get very nasty if someone started throwing rocks at you for no reason. He won't bite.'

'You can't be sure of that.'

'I'm sure. Give me the stone.' I took it and threw it in the opposite direction to the dog. Needless to say, the dog did not attack and although it was still there when we came out of the house, it didn't even bother to bark.

The words dogs do understand are the ones that are thrown at them most, and they learn the ones associated with pleasant activities like food and exercise more quickly than the pro-hibitive ones. Well, wouldn't you?

Our old terrier Bob became such a nuisance when the words

'walk' or 'sweets' were dropped into the conversation that my parents took to only saying the actual word if it were to be applied to Bob and at all other times to spell it out. He very quickly learned W-A-L-K and S-W-E-E-T-S, and although they dropped the practice after he learned to spell, he never forgot. Years after, if anyone said, 'I'm going for a W-A-L-K. Does anyone want to come too?' he was there, his whole body saying yes, please. Of course, the likelihood is that prior to spelling the word, the speaker had quite unconsciously glanced at Bob a few times, alerting him to the fact that something was up. After all, the only reason for spelling it at all was to see whether he'd forgotten.

The Survival Instinct ——————————

It isn't only dogs who have forebodings, who 'pick up bad vibes', so to speak. At one time, when I was in my mid-teens, we had some fourteen cats, all of them female, none of them spayed and consequently we had never-ending litters of kittens. The reason we had so many females was quite simply because there were no homes for them and neither of my parents approved of 'interfering' with Nature. This is a nicely sentimental attitude but, with so many cats, it inevitably led to the need for a far greater level of interference than merely spaying. My father decreed that they must all be put down. What's more, he booked the vet. My mother and I pleaded to be allowed to keep two and he relented. We selected a pretty ginger female of limited fertility, which may or may not have had something to do with her colour, and the very old former stray who started us off and who now had no teeth and never left the house anyway. Everything else was to go – and this time we knew he meant it.

The day the vet was due, no cats were allowed out. The two we were keeping were put safely in a basket so that they weren't taken by mistake. That left twelve cats to go. One by one they were fetched from their cosy seats by the living-room fire and were dispatched. At last there were eleven dead cats on the sitting-room floor. Eleven. Not twelve.

'Perhaps you miscounted,' the vet suggested.

We looked at the bodies and shook our heads. We could see which one was missing. There was no sign of Tigger, a tabby who had been one of the old cat's first litter. We went round the house calling her, but there was no response. It seemed that, careful as we had been, she must have slipped out that morning.

The vet wasn't going to wait indefinitely so he packed his bag. 'Give me a ring when you find her,' he told my father. 'Then I'll pop in.' But to my mother, who showed him to the door, he winked. 'I bet I don't get a call,' he said.

He was right. He had barely left the house when Tigger appeared, very composed and covered in soot. Sensing something wrong, she had hidden in one of the bedroom chimneys. My father conceded, without too much reluctance, that any cat with that much initiative deserved to live. He also agreed that in future cats should be spayed. He was, in fact, rather more upset by the whole business than he would admit, and much more than we were.

My mother and I both had the let-out that the decision wasn't ours, but I don't think that's the whole reason. I have observed that people who have been brought up with animals have a much more realistic acceptance that death, and not only 'natural' death, is sometimes inevitable. People without that background, and especially those brought up in towns, have a much more sentimental view including, currently, the idea that animals, like people, have some sort of 'right' to live. Actually, nothing has a 'right' to live, including humans – if we did, then we'd never die. Life is a privilege and if we deprive others of it, it should be for a good reason and with the minimum of pain or distress. From which you will correctly deduce that I am not a vegetarian. I will happily shoot and eat a rabbit. But I have more than once picked up from the road-side a rabbit in an advanced stage of myxomatosis and driven it twenty miles to the vet to be humanely put down. Suffering is inexcusable, slaughter is not necessarily so.

Canine Clairvoyance ——————————

There have been occasions when this instinct that all was not as it should be has been to my own advantage. One of these was when I took Aninrak to North Wales to be mated. We arrived very late and booked into a small pub that did bed-and-breakfast. Obviously, season or no season, Aninrak had to go out for a quick walk before we went to bed and the pub recommended a park not very far away. It was midnight. I am not of a nervous disposition anyway and thirty years ago one was in any case far less conscious of any need to be nervous. I think that even if I had been, the company of a large dog would have allayed any apprehensions – advisedly so, as it turned out.

We had barely entered the park when Aninrak became very edgy. I attributed this to our being in a strange place. Then it became clear from the way she kept looking back over her shoulder that something had caught her attention. That was easily enough explained: she was in season and it would hardly be surprising if some local dog had picked up her scent and followed us here. No-one in their right mind lets an in-season bitch off the lead in a public place, and I was no exception. I had no need to worry about that.

When she began to utter a few loud growls, audible, I imagine, only to me, I began to look around and it wasn't long before I spotted the object of her attention. It was certainly not a dog. No dog – not even a Great Dane – has a head that can be seen above a five-feet-tall shrub. Not unless it walks about on its hind legs, that is. No, it was a man.

I told myself that, since I was perfectly legitimately in the park at midnight, there was no reason why he shouldn't be, too. Maybe he was coming home from a late shift, or an evening with friends. Maybe. Common-sense told me that while someone going home late at night might not be in any particular hurry and therefore might perhaps stroll, they are unlikely to *lurk*, and this man was definitely lurking. Once I'd located him, I kept an eye on him and never once did I see him in the open; he was always behind one shrub or another.

Aninrak meanwhile became increasingly concerned and her growling – something I had never heard her do before, incidentally – became louder and more prolonged. I took her advice and we made our way back to the pub.

I had a not dissimilar experience with Kash. Like most Malamutes he regards people as long-lost friends and greets them accordingly. Until the following incident occurred, I'd have said he was totally undiscriminating in his attitude but I would have been wrong.

I had stopped at a motorway service station for petrol and Kash was curled up in the back of the van, invisible from outside. As I pulled away from the pumps, a pleasant-looking young man and his backpack approached me.

As he opened his mouth to speak, Kash suddenly leapt to his feet behind me, leaned over and, with his muzzle as close to the partly open passenger-window as he could get it, roared.

It wasn't a growl and it wasn't a bark. It was an indisputable roar. And he meant it.

The young man leapt back as if he'd been shot and I can't say I blame him. Not that it made any difference because he wouldn't have been given a lift in any case, but I've often wondered just what it was that so alarmed the dog. I'm quite sure it wasn't the backpack because Kash had seen them before and has seen them since without any such reaction. (They alarm many dogs because the carrier presents a misshapen and therefore 'inhuman' outline to the dog – which is why coalmen and postmen are more likely to be attacked than milkmen.) Kash certainly never acted like that again.

He was, however, much more of a guard dog at night than he ever was during daylight hours. I lived in a cottage that backed on to open pasture and Kash's kennel was in the lee of the hedge bordering my garden. The village was more or less at the junction of three large agricultural estates and the fields were rich in game. Every so often I would be woken by Kash making a deep-throated baying sound, somewhere between a howl and a bark yet quite different from either and not one of his normal utterances. If I peered out of the window, there was a good chance I would catch sight of the pinpoint glow of a cigarette the other side of the hedge. Undoubtedly a prowler of some sort.

My neighbour opposite, a farmer whose family had lived in the village for generations, told me once that when he heard that particular baying, so unlike the usual noises my dogs made (and they were normally silent at night, anyway) he took down his shotgun and went out to investigate. It was always poachers. If they were strangers, he sent them packing. If he knew them, he suggested they operate a bit further off. It was a pity he was away on holiday when the nearby pub was burgled – Kash warned the whole village something was up that night, but no-one bothered to investigate.

As a matter of fact, Aninrak and Timber got rid of burglars one night. Inadvertently, it's true, and certainly through no sixth sense. It was when I lived in a New Town, on one of those stupid estates designed by men, with vehicular access at the back (no housewife wants any visitors entering the house through the kitchen) while the front, landscaped gardens and all, only provided pedestrian access. Front doors consisted of two large panes of clear glass in a frame and the stairs went off the hall at a right-angle so that they couldn't be seen by anyone peering through the front door.

After we had been there about six months, there was a change of milkman. The replacement could have been described as chatty, but that would be the charitable adjective. He was just plain nosey. Now if there's one thing I loathe, it's people asking me all sorts of questions about things that are by no conceivable stretch of the imagination any of their business. It isn't a form of curiosity from which I suffer, so I don't pry myself and I get very wary when others do. Especially when they ask me where the dogs are kept at night. Alarm bells rang.

'Hardly important, I should think,' I said curtly enough to shut most people up.

Not our new milkman. 'Well, I was saying to my friend the other day, a visitor just wouldn't know where to expect them.'

'Precisely,' I said, took my change and closed the door.

He didn't stick the job long – only a matter of weeks – and his replacement was far more interested in completing his rounds than in chatting, and apart from feeling that it was in general an improvement, I gave the matter no further thought.

Until a couple of weeks later, that is. Aninrak and Timber both slept in my bedroom, the older bitch on the bed, the younger one on the floor. They woke me up in the middle of the night by the simple expedient of jumping on me and once my eyes were open I realised that they were both sitting, stiffly awake, staring with ear-tensed interest at the closed door.

At that stage I was more interested in their behaviour than in considerations of anything else but I soon became aware that they were not actually interested in the door so much as the noises coming from beyond it. To be specific, the sound of someone trying to open a downstairs window at the front of the house.

I froze. What did I do now? The telephone was downstairs in the sitting-room which was clearly visible through the front door.

Then there was a brief silence and when the noise resumed it was at the front door itself. The dogs' interest intensified. I opened the bedroom door and the two of them went cascading down the stairs and bounded up to the front door.

When the noise of their elephantine paws had stopped, I heard the welcome sound of footsteps running away down the path. Little did the intending intruder know that they had almost certainly planned only to invite him in for coffee! I have no evidence to support my belief that it was the former milkman; I didn't go down; I saw no-one. But I don't have the slightest doubt about it, either.

Malamutes so rarely make any noise at all that it would be no use relying on one to give you warning of intruders: the examples I've cited were all exceptions. German Spitz make better watch-dogs but they don't discriminate and I swear some, like Teazle, start barking the moment someone in Outer Mongolia even thinks about visiting. The Chow is another matter altogether. He barks rarely, which is just as well because it's a very peculiar noise, not unlike a rusty hinge grating open. He does, however, discriminate. Regular visitors – the milkman, the postman, the coalman – he ignores. Similarly, he knows which irregular visitors are going to be invited in and doesn't bother to tell me they're there. (The German Spitz do that. Why waste his breath?) Strangers are another matter, and especially strangers at night.

When I first had him, this led to misunderstandings. He was eighteen months old and would suddenly bark for what at first seemed no accountable reason. Then I realised that he barked when the lights in the cottage opposite were switched on. Why should such an everyday occurrence alarm him? Then it dawned on me that for him that's just what it wasn't. His breeder didn't have mains electricity. When the generator was switched on the lights came up slowly and the generator was in any case switched off when they went to bed and they relied on torches. From the kennels Tidy had only ever seen a gradual increase in light and what worried him was the sudden snapping on of a light where previously there had been none.

Chows have the reputation of being rather nasty. I'm told that twenty years ago this was a deserved reputation. It certainly isn't so today but it still lingers in the minds of people with no first-hand knowledge of the breed. Like the dealer who came to buy my old sitting-room suite. The gates of that house were almost impossible to open from the outside and Tidy came with me to let the man in.

He looked at the dog doubtfully. 'Is he all right?' he asked. 'He's fine,' I replied.

Tidy followed him up the drive very closely indeed. Had it been his own dog, and not a Chow – a notoriously difficult breed to train – one would have said it was walking to heel.

The dealer looked down and hesitated. 'Are you sure this dog's safe?' he asked.

I thought it might be unwise to be too emphatic. 'Let's put it this way,' I said. 'As long as I'm happy, he's happy.'

That assurance was a visible consolation but in truth, Tidy was only being polite. One escorts one's guests.

All the same, Tidy is the one dog I take serious notice of. He rarely barks and when he does, it means something's not right. When Tidy barks, I pick up a Sabatier knife and investigate. Tidy is this household's real guard dog.

Feeling for Felix ————————————

One of the most potentially tragic instances of a dog 'picking up vibes' concerned a German Spitz I bred, known as Felix. I sold him to another breeder, an experienced and very kind woman with whom he had an excellent home – until he started barking. Some German Spitz are persistent barkers, and Felix was one of them. The owner didn't mind but her neighbours did and she had no desire to be forced to get rid of her other dogs, so Felix had to go. He came back to me, and she was heart-broken.

He was a lovely dog to look at. He was house-trained, lead-trained and obedient, but there was no denying he was a bit of a barker. He was with me for about three months when a pet-home came along that seemed ideal. I explained why his original owner had been unable to keep him, but that was not seen as a problem and I also made it very clear, as I always do, that I would have him back if things didn't work out. I explained to the new owner that dogs were not unlike children and that, from the dog's point of view, she was the third home in a relatively short space of time and, like a child who has had several foster-homes, he might well exhibit signs of insecurity.

Initially she was delighted. Then her husband, who had been working away, came home and objected to the fact that the dog was unclean in the house. This was something I had been unaware of but, since they had a small child, it was obviously important.

I told them – truthfully – that he had been thoroughly clean when he was with me. I telephoned the previous owner and she expressed surprise: he had house-trained very quickly and had never back-slid. I duly passed this on to the new owners and, although they were very polite, I could sense that they didn't believe a word of it.

I reminded them of what I had originally said, comparing Felix to a foster-child, and pointed out that his present behaviour should be regarded in much the same light as a child starting to bed-wet. I said that I thought the best way to deal with it was to try to pretend it didn't matter and to clean up after him without comment.

I was not surprised when I eventually received a tearful phone call saying that she could stand it no longer, and would I take Felix back. This was a Sunday evening and in those days I worked during the week, and they lived a long way off. Naturally I said I would have him but I asked whether she thought they could stick with it until the next weekend.

'Oh, yes,' she said, 'I think we can take one more week of it.'

'Whatever you do, don't put him down,' I pleaded. 'If you can't take it, put him into a boarding kennel and I'll reimburse you.' I knew all too well that people who have made up their mind to get rid of a dog will sometimes take quite unjustifiedly drastic steps.

She was horrified. 'Oh, we wouldn't do that. No, he'll be all right here until the weekend.'

Her husband rang me later to say they would be over on the Sunday afternoon and I resigned myself to the idea of being stuck with Felix since another change of home was clearly not in his best interests.

On Saturday the phone went again. I recognised Felix's owner's voice straight away. 'You're going to think I'm a complete fool,' she began, apprehensively.

'You haven't put him down!' I exclaimed.

'Good heavens, no. It's nothing like that. It's ... well ... well, would you mind if we kept him?'

I am not often lost for words, but I was on that occasion with the result that there was a long pause before I responded. 'But I thought you couldn't take any more,' I said.

'I know, but he's so sweet.'

'And dirty.'

'But that's the funny thing. I know you won't believe this, but ever since we made up our minds to bring him back, he's been completely clean. I know it sounds silly, but there hasn't been a mistake since last Sunday.'

'How does your husband feel about it?' I wasn't entirely convinced that he wasn't the fly in the ointment.

'He's delighted. He's always been very fond of him, you know. It's just that he couldn't stand the dirt, not with a small child in the house. Can I keep him?'

'Of course you can. I'm delighted he's settled down at last. And you know where I am if there are any other problems.'

'I can't get over it. I just don't understand it,' she went on. 'It was so sudden.'

I had no problem understanding it. To the natural apprehension about a new dog had been added the irritation at his initial lapses from cleanliness when faced with yet another new home. As the irritation turned to annoyance and the annoyance to anger, the dog's insecurity grew by the day and with it, his apparent lack of house-training. Once the owners had made up their minds to get rid of him and a date had been set, the pressure was off them – OK, so he was dirty; only another week to put up with it. They relaxed. It didn't really matter any more. Poor Felix sensed that they were no longer angry, or worried, and he, too, relaxed. He simply reverted to his normal behaviour.

I'm delighted to report that not only was there no further trouble, but the owners became interested in showing and Felix did well in the show-ring and at stud.

Schani Shan't ——————————————

Not only are dogs quick both to learn and to pick up vibes, they're pretty good at cottoning on very fast to something they don't much like and then retraining their owner to do it *their* way. Schani, a German Spitz, was a case in point.

Until I moved to my present house, all but three of my house-dogs slept in the kitchen. The three slept in my bedroom. The new house, however, had a centrally heated barn, ideal for partitioning off into dogs' sleeping quarters. Everyone trotted along there quite happily each night – except Schani, who went with great reluctance after the first night. After three nights, he simply vanished and no matter how much I went over the house, calling, there was no sign of him but I discovered that, if I locked the barn and sat by the fire for a while, when I next went into the kitchen, Schani would be curled up on the settle or in the tea-chest beside the stove. He looked as if he had been there all along but I *knew* he had been nowhere to be seen when I had been putting the others to bed. The house-dogs had free access to three rooms in this house: the kitchen, which is large and warm; the summer-room which traps the sun; and the utility room, about which the less said, the better. There was nowhere for a dog to hide, or so it seemed: the kitchen, including the stove, was fitted; it was a simple matter to look under the chairs in the summer-room; and the utility room held only a freezer and a washing-machine, both of them too close to the wall for a dog to squeeze behind.

Of course, I was wrong. Not about the equipment being too close to the wall but about the contents of the utility room. I completely disregarded the fact that one end of it was divided off into a loo, which was a self-contained room with a door that closed properly, and a shower cubicle separated from the rest of the utility room only by a curtain. Eventually the penny dropped and when I peered round the curtain, sure enough, there he was, trying to look insignificant.

Once I'd discovered his hiding-place, he tried to obscure himself still more by getting into the farthest corner and turning his back to the outside world – a variation of the legendary ostrich behaviour, I suppose.

In the end I relented. He had a knack of flattening his ears and making his dark eyes very round in his white face so that he resembled nothing so much as one of those tragically

appealing seal-pups one sees on posters. It was several days before he was prepared to trust his luck. I 'forgot' to round him up with the rest and I stopped calling him when they were safely tucked up. I also 'forgot' to close the door of the sitting-room – forbidden territory during the day. That first night it was a good hour before he sneaked surreptitiously through the door and climbed as unobtrusively as he could into an arm-chair.

Each evening the interval of time shortened and his movements became less furtive. Now, as soon as I go into the kitchen
to settle the other dogs for the night, he goes in the opposite
direction as if by right. In fact, he sleeps on the bed now, along
with Teazle and Basua. He's getting on a bit and old age has
to produce some privileges, even for a dog.

Old Dogs and New Tricks ——————————

One old dog who taught himself a new trick was Oske and, since
he figured in the first anecdote in this book, perhaps it is fitting
that he should have the last – and have it all to himself.

His owner was a lady who had had dogs all her life and who
lived in a large house near Highgate Woods. When he was
eight years old I had a long, rambling letter, the gist of which
was to ask me to have him back because she felt she could no
longer cope, a conclusion with which, having read the rest of
the letter, I felt bound to concur. I sent her a telegram to say
I'd come for the dog at the week-end and *please* keep him till
then, and another to my son at university asking him to come
home because I knew the owner had never had transport and
I envisaged one or two problems in getting a large dog into
the car.

The letter had told me that the dog had not been out for
three years because she had had a fall and couldn't go far;
neighbours' offers to take him out had been refused because
he was rare and therefore valuable and she doubted whether
they'd bring him back. I doubted it, too, though not because
of any value he might have. When we got there it was clear
that not only had Oske not been out for three years, but
neither had anyone cleaned up after him in that time. There
was no electricity because his owner had cut through the wires,
believing they were being used to spy on her and the only
water was from a standpipe outside the back-door because
the plumbers who had come to fix an internal leak had gone
off for their coffee within an hour of arriving and had never
returned.

The stench was unbelievable. I have very little sense of smell. At one inner-city school, I used to be given the dirtiest children because the staff knew that when I started to complain, it was time to call in the Social Services.... Oske's home turned my stomach. He had been well fed – that's to say, he had been given plenty of food and wasn't thin. A diet of meat and eggs is unbalanced, however; a dog needs plenty of carbohydrates as well as protein, so he had no fur down his spine and a nasty open sore on his neck. Lack of exercise had allowed his claws to grow to such an extent that his pasterns – the equivalent of our wrists – were flat on the ground.

Oske had been her sole companion since the death of her sister several years before and his owner was in tears as we loaded him, with some difficulty, into the van. I could only assure her she had done the right thing and promise to send her some photos of him, which I later did, to her obvious delight now that she had been moved by Social Services to a large mental hospital where a dog was out of the question.

The sister had bred Pekinese and since the two of them agreed that Oske and the Pekes should be kept apart, the Pekes were upstairs and Oske was down. The Pekes went into the back garden and Oske into Highgate Woods. Why, when the Pekes were gone, didn't he go into the garden? You may well ask, since it would at least have prevented the house from getting into the state it was in. The reason was simple. Access to the garden was via the basement, which meant going down a flight of stairs and Oske, who had spent his life on the ground floor, couldn't manage stairs.

On the way home, we stopped off at the vet's just to make sure none of the many things wrong with him were infectious, and to collect half a gallon of medicated shampoo with which to drown the smell as well as disinfect him generally.

Poor old Oske. He took it all in his bewildered stride and when we finally shut ourselves in the sitting-room for a breath of relatively fresh air and a well deserved pot of tea, he was left to potter about in the kitchen and hall.

Now it so happens that stairs, which are an obstacle human beings take, if you'll forgive the pun, in their stride, present a formidable one to dogs. Try coming down yours on all fours and you'll have some idea why. Dealing with them is a skill best learned young but, while puppies very soon learn to get *up*stairs without too much difficulty, coming down is something else. They whimper and whine and if you try to force the issue by dragging them down the first two or three steps, they tell the whole neighbourhood you're murdering them. You're wasting your time anyway, because they usually solve the problem – eventually – themselves. I've had several Malamutes who have gained the confidence they needed by the simple expedient of grasping my ankle firmly in their mouth and using it as a crutch to come downstairs. It can be painful and it certainly doesn't do anything for one's tights, but it seems to work and once they've acquired the necessary confidence, they never revert to it again. Older dogs like Oske have problems.

Our stairs went up from the hall where Oske was, along the wall that separated them from the sitting-room. Imagine our utter surprise, when we heard the unmistakable sounds of someone – or something – negotiating the stairs. First we heard a clumsy, hesitant clump, clump as Oske tackled the stairs for the first time, obviously taking one cautious step at a time. When it sounded like he'd reached the top, there was a long pause. A very long pause.

'D'you think we ought to go and help him?' my son asked.

'No,' I replied. 'Give him a bit longer.'

Oske filled in some of his uncertainty by plodding along the landing and investigating the bedrooms and bathroom. Then he returned to the head of the stairs and there was another long pause.

Then he decided to tackle the stairs.

Clump.

Clump.

Pause.

Clump.

Slither, slither, slither, slither, bump.

'He's done it,' I said. 'He'll go and lie down now.'

Did he, heck as like. There was another pause, a brief one this time, and off he went upstairs again, less hesitantly this time. Going up is, as I said, easier than coming down. This time there was no exploration of the upper floor. He paused, presumably to get his breath and gather his courage to the sticking point and off he went again.

Clump.

Clump.

Clump, clump, clump

Slither, slither, slither, bump. Pause.

Then he repeated the exercise again – and again, and again, and every time the clumps increased and the slithers decreased until by the end of the evening Oske had taught himself to go up and down stairs with as much ease as a dog who had done it from puppyhood.

What is it they say about not being able to teach a dog new tricks? Maybe you can't, but there's nothing to say an old dog can't teach himself one or two.